John Field and Chopin

John Field and Chopin

David Branson

St. Martin's Press

Copyright © 1972 by David Branson
All rights reserved. For information, write:
St. Martin's Press, Inc., 175 Fifth Ave., New York, N.Y. 10010
Printed in Great Britain
Library of Congress Catalog Card Number: 70-171229
First published in the United States of America in 1972

AFFILIATED PUBLISHERS: Macmillan & Company, Limited, London —
also at Bombay, Calcutta, Madras and Melbourne — The Macmillan
Company of Canada, Limited, Toronto

Contents

Prefatory Note.

Particular titles of works, books, and some foreign words where less generally in use as an acquired part of the English language, or for emphasis, are italicized. More general titles, etc., are not. For example, Rondo, Polonaise and Polacca, but *Rondo Favori, Alla Polacca, Air Russe Varié*.

Introduction.

... A decorative passage from one of the first two editions of Field's Nocturne in C minor, when it appeared as the third of *Three Romances.* A set of *Three Nocturnes,* in which it was No. 2, was issued by another publisher in the same year, 1814. This passage (with a little extra material which preceded it) was replaced in in the Nocturne by a simple restatement of the theme.

John Field, 1782–1837.   Frédéric Chopin, 1810–1849.

I.

In the latter part of the 18th century the pianoforte was to undergo a special development as an expressive instrument.

Already, Christofori's new action, invented in the first years of the century and perfected by 1720, had given it the possibility, which the harpsichord had not possessed, of tonal gradations from soft to loud, and the sustaining pedal, added in 1777, allowed the holding of harmonies and the playing of melodies over sustained harmonies, thus bringing within the scope of the instrument a whole new range of sonorities and subtleties of expression.

This increased capacity was reflected in the works of the later classical composers, Beethoven in particular, while music awaited the first poet of the instrument, who, with an ear tuned to its finest nuances, would develop not only its melodic and decorative resources, but its technical also, in the way that Paganini did with the violin.

Now, along with the piano's advanced possibilities in colour and sonority, a parallel development was to occur in the music written for it.

The composer who comes most readily to mind as a poetic writer for the piano, one who particularly grasped and explored its possibilities, is of course Frédéric Chopin. But there was an earlier composer who did this in very similar terms (a glance at the introductory example will give an initial idea of how similar), but whose music, despite a little recent revival, is still largely forgotten. This was John Field, all of whose works, like those of Chopin, involved the instrument. Considered the greatest pianist of his time, he was during his lifetime and for a considerable period afterwards a composer of equal renown.

Field was born on July 26th, 1782, in Dublin, where the family lived in Golden Lane, and was baptised at St. Werburgh's Church, in Werburgh Street, on September 30th of that year. Both his father and grandfather were musicians, his father, Robert Field, being a violinist in the orchestra of the Theatre Royal, in Crow Street, and his grandfather on his father's side, also John, an organist at a Dublin church and a successful teacher of both organ and pianoforte. His mother's name, given on the baptismal certificate, was Grace. Her maiden name would appear to be lost to us, unless she is the same

1

person as an Ann Dunn, to marry whom a Robert Field applied for a licence in 1780, this fact being recorded in the *Index to the Acts or grant books, and the original wills of the diocese of Dublin to the year 1800.* The Index alone remains, the actual volumes were destroyed in an explosion in the Public Record Office in 1922. I have found no mention of his mother's name by any writer on Field (not that there has been very much written about him), and how long she lived is not known to us. So whether she was Ann Grace Dunn (or Grace Ann), or whether the husband of Ann Dunn was another Robert Field must remain, unless any further detail comes to light later, a matter for conjecture. A daughter was born to Robert and Grace Field in 1788, whom they named Ann. Again, I have seen no mention by any writer of the composer having brothers or sisters.

Field began to study the piano under his grandfather at the age of seven (some writers say five), his father supervising his practice. The senior Field lived in the same house as the younger family. The grandfather being a harsh teacher and the father an equally harsh supervisor, Field's earlier period of study seems not to have been too happy, and he even ran away from home on one occasion.

In 1781 Field was sent to Tommaso Giordani for lessons, and was now displaying such early virtuosity that Giordani billed him to appear at three 'Spiritual Concerts' which he arranged at Dublin's Rotunda during Lent of 1792, at the second of which Field played a concerto by Giordani. The first of these concerts, on March 24th, was ostensibly his debut, but he had previously appeared as one of a number of 'musical children' at Master Tom Cooke's benefit concert on February 14th, at the Exhibition Rooms, William Street. For the Giordani concerts, Field, being nearly ten, was advertised as eight years of age. His playing received high praise from press and public.

In 1792 and 1793 Field produced his first compositions: an arrangement for piano solo of the Irish air *Go to the Devil and shake yourself;* two Rondos for piano on Giordani's songs *Since then I'm doomed* and *Slave, bear the sparkling goblet round;* and *Signora del Caro's Hornpipe with Variations* ——— all being much admired by audiences of the time. An Irish edition of the first in 1793 is mentioned, and a following printing of the other three, all said to have been reprinted in England by Longman and Broderip in 1795, and again by Clementi and Company in 1810, the year in which Clementi issued the first three Sonatas, Op. 1. Of the four the *Hornpipe* is traceable today in the 1795 edition, *Since then I'm doomed* not until an edition of 1818, and the other two not at all.

During the Summer of 1893 Field's father was invited to become leader of the orchestra at the Bath concerts, and the family moved to England, to that city. In December of that year they moved again, to London, Robert Field taking up an appointment as a violinist at the Haymarket Theatre.

In London Field was apprenticed to Muzio Clementi for a fee of 100 guineas, becoming both his pupil and a salesman in Clementi's London shop, part of his duties being to play over music to the customers and especially to display the firm's pianos. Field was kept at this for five years. Clementi, however, did not overlook his development as a performer, and he first appeared in London in May 1794, playing a Clementi Sonata. Haydn, Dussek and Cramer made great predictions for his future. At this time he also studied the violin, along with the young Geo. Fredk. Pinto, under Salomon.

In 1799, on February 7th, he played his own first Concerto at a Pinto benefit concert at the Haymarket Theatre. One wonders if his father was perhaps in the orchestra. In its report two days later the Morning Chronicle mentioned the young man as having been, at fifteen years of age, "esteemed by the best judges one of the finest performers in the kingdom, and his astonishing ability on this occasion proved how justly he was entitled to the distinction." The Concerto, too, received high praise. A later performance of this Concerto which attracted special attention was one he gave at Covent Garden on February 20th, 1801.

In August, 1802, Clementi took Field to Paris, where his playing of Bach and Handel Fugues, and also works by his teacher, made a sensation. The two musicians then proceeded to Germany and Russia, Field's appearances being accompanied by a gradual crescendo of praise until, as might be expected, the master became jealous of the pupil's success. Yet not only had Clementi received a worthwhile sum for Field's apprenticeship, but the latter had earned good fees for performances and from giving lessons, all of which was to benefit Clementi particularly, who, nevertheless, kept his pupil short of food and, it was said, without even an overcoat to protect him through the Russian winter. Clementi's primary reason for taking Field abroad, it seems, was not so much to present him as a virtuoso as to use him to display the Clementi pianos, and when the two reached St. Petersburg in December, 1802, Clementi at once opened a showroom for the sale of the firm's instruments, with Field employed in his old capacity. Thus the praise everywhere accorded his protegé as performer must have no little disconcerted him, switching the accent as it did from the pianos to the player.

Probably the most familiar picture of Field (if any is really familiar) is that given by Spohr in his *Autobiography,* in which he mentions visiting Clementi and his pupil in St. Petersburg in 1802. The autobiography takes the form of later reminiscences and reflections around quotations from Spohr's earlier diaries, which he gives in inverted commas in the text. Though it presents Clementi in a not very favourable light (a reputation which has survived), Spohr's is a direct observation of the two musicians, giving a pertinent if not very comfortable picture of Field at that time, so I give the whole passage.

"Clementi, 'a man in his best years, of an extremely lively disposition, and very engaging manners,' liked much to converse with me '(in French, which from my great practice in St. Petersburg I soon spoke pretty fluently)' and often invited me after dinner to play at billiards. In the evening I sometimes accompanied him after dinner to his large pianoforte warehouse, where Field was often obliged to play for hours, to display the instruments to the best advantage to the purchasers. The diary speaks with great satisfaction of the technical perfection and the 'dreamy melancholy' of that young artist's execution. I have still in recollection the figure of the pale, overgrown youth, whom I have never seen since. When Field, who had outgrown his clothes, placed himself at the piano, stretched out his arms over the keyboard, so that his sleeves shrunk up nearly to his elbows, his whole figure appeared awkward and stiff in the highest degree; but as soon as his touching instrumentation began, everything else was forgotten, and one became all ear. Unhappily, I could not express my emotion and thankfulness to the young man otherwise than by a silent pressure of the hand, for he spoke no other language, but his mother tongue.

Even at that time, many anecdotes of the remarkable avarice of the rich Clementi were related, which had greatly increased in latter years when I again met him in London. It was generally reported that Field was kept on very short allowance by his master, and was obliged to pay for the good fortune of having his instruction with many privations. I myself experienced a little sample of Clementi's true Italian parsimony, for one day I found teacher and pupil with turned up sleeves, engaged at the washtub, and Clementi advised me to do the same, as washing in St. Petersburg was not only very expensive, but the linen suffered greatly from the method used in washing it."

When Clementi left Russia in 1803, Field remained behind, settling in St. Petersburg. He was offered a court position by Prince Orloff, but declined it. He was quickly to become the most esteemed pianist in Russia and the most sought after teacher, as Clementi found when he returned for a visit a year later. The nobility extended to Field both their patronage and their friendship, and with them he attended the opera and the important social occasions, when he was not performing at the latter. No doubt at the opera he heard the romantic and embellished melodies which were to come out under his fingers over his flowing basses in the Nocturnes and the *cantilene* sections in the Concertos.

Though Spohr wrote in the passage quoted that he never saw Field again, he mentions a little later, while describing events taking place in 1803, that "This evening Field played as well as Herr Eck, and in truth wonderfully. At two o'clock, the company sat down to supper, and we did not arrive home till past four o'clock." Franz Eck was Spohr's violin teacher, whom he had accompanied to Russia, and the date, which he does not mention for this particular evening, would seem, from dates he gives for prior and after events, to have been either in late February or March. The "as well as" has, of course, the meaning of "besides" and is not intended to mean "equally as well," as might appear from a first reading.

Over the next few years Field was so much feted that be became pleasure-loving and eccentric, forgetting appointments for lessons and leading a thoroughly Bohemian life, during which he had a succession of love affairs. In 1810[1] he married one of his best pupils, a Mademoiselle Percheron de Mouchy,[2] nicknamed ' Percheretta ' because of her coquettish disposition. March 10th and 14th 1812, find them giving concerts together in Moscow, the first being a benefit concert for the orchestra of the Imperial Theatre and the second a performance at the house of a noblewoman, Princess Trubitsky. Though the marriage was not a particularly happy one, a son, Adrien, was born in 1919, the mother taking him with her when the couple separated not long after.

A Field Concerto and a Quintet are mentioned in a letter of 1807 from Clementi, then in Austria, to Collard, in London, as expected by Clementi's for publication, in payment or part payment for a grand piano. The Concerto meant is probably No. 1, which was eventually first published by Breitkopf and Härtel in 1815.

During all these years Field's reputation steadily increased, and he

---

[1] While earlier writers state 1808, there is support now for 1810, with the marriage several years impending. W. H. Grattan Flood, in his *John Field of Dublin—A Brief Memoir*, gives the priest's name, Szyruk, with marriage 1808 and separation 1813.
[2] Full surname; the ' de Mouchy ' usually dropped and there being no record of her first name.

counted notable names among his pupils: Glinka, the founder of the Russian National Opera and Nationalist School (of composition); Charles Neate, the English pianist and composer; de Kontski, Polish prodigy who later settled and taught in Paris; Vertowski, Russian composer of operas mostly after Italian models, whose *Thief of Askold* enjoyed a long popularity in the 18th century; Charles Mayer, German pianist and composer of a large number of piano pieces, one of whose Mazurkas was included as by Chopin in the first Klindworth edition of the latter's works; and Madame Szymanowska, whose children Chopin was later to teach.

In 1810 or thereabouts Field's *Divertissement* with String Quartet No. 1 in E major, of which the *Midi* Rondo is a later shorter solo version, was published in Russia, and the *Divertissement* with Quartet No. 2 in A ——— *Pastorale* and *Rondeau* (Nocturne No. 8 being the *Pastorale* shortened by 34 bars and reshaped), was published, similarly in Russia, in 1811. The *Rondeau* ——— with one or two small differences, the main being an alteration of the opening bars of the theme ——— appeared separately later as the Rondo (or *Rondo Favori*) No. 2, the earlier solo version of the first *Divertissement* being *Rondo Favori* No. 1. French and German editions of the first *Divertissement* followed in 1812 and by 1816 it was in print in England, Italy and Austria also, and of the second English and French editions appeared in 1811 and 1812 respectively, the spread of Field's earlier works being thus extensive. The *Fantasie on Martín y Soler's 'Andante'* appeared, published in Leipzig, in 1812. The fourth Sonata was published in Russia in 1812, having Italian and German editions in 1813 and 1814 respectively, and the Rondo in A flat, as Quintet in Russia in 1812 (and piano solo later). A number of other works, with editions from Russia to England, appeared during these years. The *Air Russe Favori Varié 'Kamarinskaya'*, in B flat, which exhibited a striking technical pattern that Chopin made use of in his *Là ci darem* Variations, also in B flat, was published both in Russia and England in 1813.

The first three Nocturnes were published by Peters in Leipzig in 1814, and a set of *Three Romances*, consisting of the *Pastorale* from the second *Divertissement* in the shorter Nocturne version and Nocturnes No. 1 in E flat and No. 2 in C minor, by Breitkopf and Härtel, also in Leipzig and also in 1814. Field would seem at first not to have been quite decided on his title of 'Nocturne' for these pieces, especially as the present Nocturne No. 9 in E flat appeared also as a Romance, published by Breitkopf, in 1816. As noted in the Introduction to this book, the passage given there occurs in the Romance edition of the C minor Nocturne (to judge from the inclusion of the earlier *Pastorale,* very likely Field's first version of this piece), being replaced in the piece as a Nocturne in its 1814 and all later editions by a simple restatement of the theme in place of this, its embellished form. At the time these Nocturnes and Romances appeared, already exhibiting to the full the facets of Field's *cantilena* and the very personal flavour of his musical thought, Chopin was a boy of four years old (and only one year when the *Pastorale* was first published as part of the second *Divertissement*).

Breitkopf followed the publication of the first Concerto in 1815 with that of the second, third and fourth in 1816, the A flat Quintet (not to be confused with the A flat Rondo, Quintet and piano solo) being published by them in the same year. Nocturnes Nos. 4 and 5 were in print in Russia and Germany in 1817, the year which saw the publication of the fifth Concerto, *L'Incendie par l'Orage* and Nocturne No. 6 was printed in Russia in 1817 and in Germany in 1818. The latter is the same as the slow movement of the Concerto No. 6, transposed from E into F major, the Concerto itself being published not until 1823 in Russia and Germany, and 1824 in France. On the evidence of the Nocturne, the Concerto, or at least its first two movements, had very likely been written by 1817. Field's Nocturnes Nos. 7 and 8 were in print in Russia in 1821 and Germany in 1822 (No. 8 being then the E minor ––– now No. 10 in Peters and most other editions, while No. 8 is the shorter solo form of the *Pastorale* from the second *Divertissement,* which was published as the first of the *Three Romances* in 1814). Field had already performed the first movement of the Concerto No. 7, with its exquisite G major central interlude, in Moscow in 1822, though the whole work was not published till 1834. Thus the major part of his output was not only in existence but in print before Chopin's Opus 1 was published in 1825.

In 1822 Field settled in Moscow. There he became very friendly with Hummel, whose works after this time (and somewhat before it ––– a change in his style having taken place from a drier to a more romantic viewpoint) would suggest that Field's pianistic ideas had a considerable influence on him. Field made a lot of money from his concerts, commanding higher fees than any other performer, and gathered an increasingly large teaching connection, pupils coming from far afield merely to say they had received lessons from him. But during the eighteen-twenties his Bohemian habits led him especially into intemperance, causing him to neglect engagements and to the detriment of his health, while his love affairs, having been the gossip of St. Petersburg during his earlier years there, now scandalized Moscow. Twice his death was reported: in 1828 and 1831. On the latter occasion he published a tart reply, and the paper concerned printed a lively rejoinder to the effect that, though it was understood Monsieur Field still lived, he could not easily be coaxed to exhibit his powers, and that if he could conquer his reluctance, Europe might still expect to hear from him. Though in the 1820's his production and publication of new works had declined, reprints and other editions of the previous, and the acclaim accorded them, had continued, and though he himself had for so long not been heard outside Russia as a pianist, his reputation had all the time increased.

Field did conquer his reluctance, and later in that year (1831) he accepted an invitation from the Philharmonic Society to come to London where, on February 27th, 1832, he played his Concerto No. 3 in E flat. He played at a Haydn Centenary concert on March 31st, other performers being Cramer and Moscheles. The last-named, hearing Field a year earlier, had described "his enchanting legato, his tenderness and elegance and his beautiful touch." During this visit Clementi died, and Field was one of the chief mourners at his funeral at Westminster Abbey on March 29th. In May, at a reception given by Moscheles, he met Mendelssohn, who was delighted by the Irishman's playing, and he was now urged by friends in Paris to follow up his renewed success in London by giving recitals there. The first was on December 25th, 1832, in the Salle of the Conservatoire, and the second and third were at the Pape Salon on January 20th and February 3rd, 1833. He was received in Paris even more enthusiastically than in London, though Chopin had been giving a series of recitals there a few months earlier. Most later writers state that Field's powers were beginning to fail him at this time, but this opinion is not at all borne out by the reviews, according to the writers of which his abilities remained at their peak until ill-health overcame him in Naples in 1834, at the end of two years of travelling and performing. Of the first Paris concert the French critic Fétis wrote describing the audience's response as "a veritable delirium," and said that whoever had not heard "this great pianist" could have no idea of "the marvellous mechanism of his fingers ——— such that the greatest difficulties appear to be the simplest things," and that Field was "not less astonishing in the art of attack as in producing an infinite variety of nuances." And of the last concert, while he was less enthusiastic about the seventh Concerto, describing it as "diffuse, but full of happy ideas," he added that "the exquisite playing of M. Field more than made up in compensation."

True, Chopin, in a letter, professed himself disappointed (he had heard Field and the seventh Concerto at the last concert). He had long wished to hear the renowned Irish artist, saying that people frequently stated that his playing reminded them of Field's and asked him if he was a pupil. But Joseph d'Ortique, in his *Balcon de l'Opera*, 1833, wrote: "As a pianist Field has no rival, whether as regards genre of method. He has no adopted system and is of no school ... Field is Field ——— a school of his own. He is a native and original talent." He describes Field's playing as "exquisitely spiritual, coupled with surprising aplomb and coquetry.' D'Ortigue also wrote that, like Paganini, Field was no less remarkable in his compositions than in his playing, the hearers being thus afforded "a double study."

These Paris concerts came at the beginning of an extended tour. On February 18th, 1833, Field gave the first of two concerts in Brussels, both a great success, playing after that in Toulouse, Marseilles and Lyons ——— where his performance and the works were reviewed as equally remarkable ——— and in South Germany. In September he went to Geneva, where he gave concerts on September 30th and October 14th. The second concert was a request repeat of the first, the programme including the sixth Concerto, the *Midi* Rondo with quartet accompaniment, and a number of solo pieces. He played in Milan in November and December, where he was hailed as an artist without parallel by leading Italian critics, and from Milan he went to Florence, Venice and Naples. Again while later writers stress this as Field's period of decline, the acclaim given him in each centre does not bear out this view. The whole period from London in 1832 to Naples in 1834 saw an increase and not a decrease in his reputation. The decline was not in performance but in health. The strain of this long period of performing told on him, and his intemperate habits had not helped his stamina. He was taken ill in Naples in the Spring of 1834. There he was taken into hospital, where he had an operation for fistula.

Field lay in hospital for a year, refusing to let friends or pupils know of his condition, until a Russian noble family, the Rachmanoffs,* arrived in Naples in June, 1835. They removed him from hospital and he stayed with them first in Ischia, where the waters of the medicinal springs helped heal him, then went with them to Venice and by easy stages back to Russia.

On the way he stayed in Vienna with Czerny and, his health having considerably improved, he began writing and playing again. He gave three concerts at Vienna's Hof Theatre on August 8th, 11th

---

Grove's Dictionary gives Rayemanov. W. H. Grattan Flood gives Rachmanoff, which Alex. A. Nikolaev's biography in Russian of the composer confirms.

and 13th, 1835, writing too, it is said, a Nocturne and a new Concerto. This Concerto, a No. 8, if indeed he wrote it, is lost to us. Concerto No. 7 was offered to Breitkopf and Härtel in the second half of 1833, and published by them in 1834, a French edition appearing in the same year, and the years 1831—36 saw a renewed publication of new works which included, besides the Concerto, the *Introduction and Rondo on Blewitt's Cavatina* (1832), Nocturnes Nos. 11, 13, 14, 15 and 16 (from 1833—6), and the *Grande Pastorale* in E (1832), which without its String Quartet accompaniment became Nocturne No. 17. Dannreuther wrote of the admiration evoked by Field's "exquisite performances" in the Vienna concerts. Notwithstanding later views, he seems to have remained the supreme master of his instrument to the end.

Later that year Field returned to Moscow with the Rachmanoffs. His health had further improved and his period of sickness seemed over, until in the November of 1836 he developed bronchial trouble under the severity of the Russian winter. By Christmas it was obvious that he had not long to live, and he died on January 11th, 1837. He was given a public funeral and was buried in the Wedensky-Kirkhof in Moscow. A monument to his memory was erected by his near circle of friends together with past pupils.

There is no doubt as to the position Field occupied in his time as a performer: he was everywhere considered to be the finest. In France he was called "the Racine of the piano." He was likened to Paganini, and his playing, full of colour and expressiveness, was compared with Catalani's style of singing, it being often said that in his performing he displayed the finer taste. As a pianist Kullak considered him to be "one of the greatest masters of all time in his picturesque diffusion of light and shade, in perfect finesse allied to the utmost warmth of expression," while it is evident, too, that during his lifetime and for a considerable time afterwards, he was esteemed equally as a composer. If we cannot regard all his music in the same light today ——— his larger works especially have short-comings which to audiences accustomed to expect continuity of thought and shapeliness of form rob them of much of their impact ——— his was still one of the few truly original minds. He not only invented the Nocturne ——— how complete an invention we cannot miss from his No. 2 in C minor and No. 4 in A major ——— but brought into being, too, a whole new range of pianistic expressiveness and feeling, from the *cantilene* melodies with their opera-like embellishments in the Nocturnes and the Concertos to the bravura technical passages and devices in the latter and other works. The Romantic flavour in music came into being with

Field ——— how completely we cannot know until we examine all his works, especially the larger. The influence of his music was similarly wide ——— again we cannot know how wide until we examine it in detail.

There are so many lives of Chopin available that I am not attempting a biographical sketch here. Field is both the artist about whom and whose music too little is known and the all-too-little-acknowledged influence, particularly on Chopin. The latter subject is to occupy the remaining sections of this book.

2.

It is not unusual to hear expressed, or to see written, the opinion that Chopin was a composer whose style was so new and so personal that it owed little or nothing to the idioms of composers before him.

As it would be extremely unlikely that any composer could be without a jumping-off ground in some texture or flavour in the music which preceded him or surrounded him in his formative period, such a statement usually means that the person holding the opinion does not know where to look.

Sometimes, when influences are mentioned, we are given suggestions of more distant links with Bach: his modulating, perpetual-motion Preludes of the 'Forty-eight' influencing Chopin's Études ——— e.g. Bach's first C major Prelude into Chopin's first C major Étude and Bach's second C minor Prelude into Chopin's Étude in C minor, Op. 25, No. 12; and again, Bach's coverage of the twenty-four major and minor keys in the Preludes and Fugues suggesting to Chopin his Preludes covering the twenty-four keys. Mozart's refinement and elegance are also mentioned as an influence ——— music, in the case of both these composers, with its own beauty and integrity, but which does not yet carry any suggestion of the essential Chopin flavour.

Contemporary or near-contemporary writers on Chopin are divided between those who consider there was no influence on his style from other keyboard composers, those who mention none, those who consider there was an influence from Field's Nocturnes and/or one from Hummel and several minor composers like Cramer and Clementi (the non-keyboard influences of Polish national dances, Viennese and French salon music and Italian opera being more generally admitted ones), and one or two who hint at a wider Field influence but do either very little or nothing to illustrate this.

In the books on Chopin which I have read, only in one case have I seen an example mentioned (but not set out) which does not come from the Nocturnes.

I need to say here that, that quite apart from the inestimable amount I have learned from these books, and articles, by various writers and the solidity of their testament to Chopin's stature as a composer and interest as a man, I am looking at them in this case, and setting down some opinions from them, with the sole purpose of finding out how much or how little they have to say about Field.

To mention first some of the opinions in which Chopin is considered to stand alone as the inventor of a new keyboard sound and style, to which he was not the heir in any way from his predecessors. In *Men of Music,* published in America, Chopin is described as "The most truly original of all composers." Again, Hubert Foss, in his article in the *Radio Times* on the Centenary of Chopin's death — — — an article exceptionally perceptive of his strength and stature as a composer — — — submits finally that "his music came from nowhere but himself," that while he learnt *cantilena* from the Italian opera, "he sang it on the piano," and that "He was one of the very few original and newly inventive composers in all musical history." The *Musical Times* in its Centenary article describes him as "one of the great originators," with no mention of any influence on his style.

According Chopin the same position of isolation, Charles Fox, writing in the *Radio Times* of February 4th, 1965 — — — the BBC presenting at the time a series of recitals encompassing all or nearly all the composer's works — — — considers him to be "a man who brought an entirely new sound into keyboard music."

Alfred Einstein, in *A Short History of Music* (1936), gives Chopin a single stylistic link with Rossini's type of operatic melody, but does not mention Field at all in the volume, either in connection with the former composer or on his own account, thus crediting him with no share in the development of either Romantic or keyboard music.

Stephen P. Miźwa, in his book *Chopin* (New York, 1949), includes no mention of Field.

Casimir Wierzynski, in *The Life and Death of Chopin* (1951), mentions Field three times, but never in relation to his style and its possible influence on that of the Polish composer.

Adam Harasowski, in *The Skein of Legends around Chopin* (1967), gives short analyses of forty-two books on the composer. In these analyses the name of Field occurs once: as the teacher of Charles Mayer, a mazurka of whose found its way into the

Klindworth edition of Chopin's works. This, of course, is unlikely to be the only mention of Field in the books themselves, though it is the only one which Harasowski picked out, but it would be a likely conclusion that the forty-two writers did not to any marked degree leap to put forward a Field influence on Chopin's style.

Moritz Karasowski, in his *Chopin* (1879), mentions Field once, in saying that "Kalkbrenner, to whom Chopin played his E minor Concerto, remarked that he had "Cramer's style, but Field's touch." André Boucourechliev, in *"Chopin ––– a pictorial biography"* (1963), gives the same single mention, while adding Kalkbrenner's conclusion of his remark to the young Pole as pianist: "but that he was not sufficiently disciplined."

J. Cuthbert Hadden, in *Chopin* (1903), says: "Schumann said of him: 'He studied from the very best models: he took from Beethoven temerity and inspiration, from Schubert tenderness and feeling, from Field manual dexterity.' But this can be accepted in only the most general terms, as one would accept that Beethoven was indebted to Bach, or Pope to Spenser and Dryden." This latter remark is practically to dismiss any stylistic influence of Field's or anyone else's compositions over Chopin's.

Joan Chissell, in her book *Chopin* (1963), while she considers that "The brilliant show-pieces" he "had learnt by Hummel and Moscheles and other virtuoso composers" prompted him to compose similar himself, does not mention Field, though he might be taken to be among the "other virtuoso composers" by a reader knowing independently more of the surrounding musical scene.

Camille Bourniquel, in *Chopin* (1960), quotes Field's remark on Chopin having "the talent of the sick-room," and otherwise mentions him only in connection with Chopin and the Nocturne, saying that the latter succeeded "in giving it what it had previously lacked ––– a content." (Could Field's Nocturnes Nos. 2, 4, 12 and 17 be said to have no content? ––– I do not think so.) Bourniquel gives a seemingly unwitting clue to a musical descent (shied away from by most writers even where they see the Nocturne link) in saying of Field's pieces in the style: "His eighteen Nocturnes are the pianistic version of the *bel canto* with its search for effect ––– arpeggio chords, ornamentation, great thrills and false lyricism."

In Alan Walker's *Frédéric Chopin: profiles of the man and the musician* (1966), a volume by ten writers and himself (as writer-editor) which is a major text-book and compendium both in the discussion of detailed aspects of the composer's entire output and an immense amount of related information, while other valid influences are presented, including one from Hummel, that of Field is considered (by three writers) to be "overrated:" as being due to "the fact that he wrote nocturnes;" also since "Chopin had composed the first five of his nocturnes before he came into brief contact with him" (the 1833 meeting); and again since, in the view of one writer, the influence of his nocturnes even on Chopin's first set, Op. 9, "amounts to little more than the idea of a reflective piece having a melody in the right hand and an accompanying figure in the left." (This last, I feel, cannot adequately be maintained when, to mention a single point, Field's Nocturne No. 1 and Chopin's No. 2 have virtually the same ending: and, too, the influence of the former's Nocturnes need not be only on the latter's pieces of the same title. Of Chopin's knowledge and use of Field's music more will be said in the next section.)

Gerald Abraham, in *Chopin's Musical Style* (1949), goes markedly farther in appreciating Field's influence and gives the impression of intending to go farther than he eventually does, when he states Chopin's debt to Field in the aspect of the Nocturne basis, "of widespread left hand arpeggios, mostly in triplets, decorated with chromatic passing notes" and disposed "in more intricate shapes than the few simple formulae that had satisfied the classical composers," to be "enormous," and "not only in this aspect, *but in a score of others.*" By way of illustration he gives the throbbing chord passage from Field's Nocturne No. 5 in B flat, noting (and illustrating) its similarity to the passage which forms the basis of the middle section of Chopin's A flat Nocturne, Op. 32, No. 2, but having done this does not enlarge on what these other aspects might be.

Discussing, for instance, Chopin's first Concerto, he observes (and examples) the similarity of its opening theme to that of Hummel's first Concerto in A minor, Op. 85. But there are also a number of direct reflections of elements in Field works occurring in it.

John F. Porte, in *Chopin the Composer and his Music* (1932), which contains much practical information on points of style and technical problems met with in playing Chopin's works, goes a step further one feels than Gerald Abraham when, having called Field "a great master of the instrument who ought not to be forgotten," whose "style of playing and even of his music closely foreshadows those of Chopin," he suggests that: "Painstaking pianists of today who aspire to reputations as Chopin players would do well to become proficient in Field's Nocturnes and his Concerto. In these works we have the essential germ of the Chopin style, ..." However, he gives no examples and of the seven Concertos one presumes that

No. 2 is meant.

Edgar Stillman Kelly, in *Chopin the Composer* (New York, 1914), speaks of the Nocturne influence and gives the single mentioned (but not illustrated) example from the Field Concertos when he says of Chopin: "In his preliminary studies for the F-minor Concerto he doubtless absorbed something of Field's mood," — — of the A flat Concerto, of which he had just spoken — — — "and the young Pole's opening theme is remarkably similar to a subordinate passage in D major in the first movement of the British master's above-mentioned. But here the likeness ceases, for ... " (The D Major given is, one imagines, a printer's error for B major, there being no passage in D in the movement.)

Basil Maine, in his *Chopin* (1933), mentions Field in connection with the invention of the Nocturne, which he describes him as attaching to piano pieces "dreamy, songlike and of flexible form" adapted from the type of serenade written for wind instruments or strings, and for the influence of his piano playing on Chopin's playing style. Saying that the latter made the Nocturne peculiarly his own, he states that Field's use of the word gave "prominence to the least of his compositions, while the three Sonatas*, the seven Concertos, and the Pianoforte Quintet have fallen into obscurity." He does not suggest any similarity in the composing styles of the two musicians and mentions no influence except that Chopin's Rondo in C minor, Op. 1, reminded Schumann of Moscheles and another (unnamed) critic of Hummel's Rondos. (Under fuller examination, as in the final section of this book devoted to Field's Other Works, we get a rather different picture of the influences at work in this Rondo.)

Arthur Hedley, in *Chopin* (1947), saying that in that composer's works "Here and there we find echoes of Field," agrees that the former thought highly of the latter as a composer. He sees, though, the only material influence to be that Chopin "took the form and name of the small scale lyrical or elegiac piece to which Field gave the title of Nocturne." But having, he continues, "adopted the general idea of the Nocturne, he transformed it into something very different from the original model. Apart from one or two early efforts (such as Op. 9, No. 2) Chopin's nocturnes belong, as regards their musical content, to a world unknown to Field." (Just how much of this world, certainly as regards basic elements and, to a not inconsiderable degree, its contrasting moods also, was known to Field and, vice versa, how much of Field's world was known to and reproduced by Chopin, we may be able to judge more exactly from

*There are four.

the ensuring discussion and examples.) Arthur Hedley finds support in an opinion of the French critic, Fétis, whom he describes as being "steeped in the music of his own and previous centuries," claiming that "if Chopin's work struck *him* as being markedly original it is safe to assume that the resemblances to Field, Kalkbrenner, Hummel and others are less real than some writers would have us believe." This, of course, cannot be proved, or disproved, without producing the music.

Herbert Weinstock, the American writer, in *Chopin — — The Man and his Music* (New York, 1949), gives a concise description of the composer's surrounding musical landscape when he says: "The musical literature with which he was familiar was made up of compositions from the baroque, classic, and rococo periods; the folk, operatic and salon music of Poland; the salon music of Vienna and Paris; and the creations of such of his contemporaries as Field, Hummel, Kalkbrenner and Moscheles. I have indicated some of his adaptations and borrowings. But what a composer accepts from the general storehouse of musical creation remains less interesting than the results of that borrowing: what he adds to it and what he himself imagines and invents." True as this conclusion unquestionably is, it is nevertheless interesting to try to find the springs of a composer's style, especially when there have been thought by quite a number to be virtually no springs at all, and, too, when the music itself has the perennial fascination of Chopin's.

Calling Field a "recklessly neglected second flight master," Weinstock sees clearly Chopin's indebtedness to him in the matter of the Nocturnes and their style, while he notices no other facet of Chopin's idiom as owing anything to the Irish composer. He prints Field's Nocturne No. 5 in B flat entire to show the similarity to it of Chopin's Nocturne in A flat, Op. 32, No. 2, saying afterwards that the latter "represents a great composer using half his powers to play with the salon-music atmosphere of Hummel and Field."

It has more than once been said to me that Field was just a salon composer, the suggestion being that because of this (an imagined limitation) he is less worthy of serious consideration, and the fact that he wrote larger works with heroic and bravura aspects to them (even if they were not completely successful as works) being over-looked. Weinstock does not comment on Field possessing, or communicating to Chopin, any stronger mood. We do learn from his book, however, that Klengel, hearing Chopin play his E minor Concerto in November, 1830, compared him both as composer and virtuoso with Field.

While these various writers have contributed near-exhaustively

both to the knowledge of Chopin's life and to the general under-
standing of his works as works (commenting on such things as
rubato: how much or how little they need; on points of performance
in differing styles of pianists playing them; on their evidence of the
composer's patriotism, his melancholy and, in contrast to it, his
fire), one has to say (after a comprehensive study of Field's works)
that an important factor relating to their forming (the works of
Chopin, that is) as well as to their place in the ' ladder ' of keyboard
music is largely missing or, where touched on, only partially
explained.

Since Chopin has without question been singled out for more
attention than any other composer, it might seem unlikely for this
to happen, but perhaps (quite apart from his music) the spotlight on
him as a romantic figure — — — his student attachments, his affair
with George Sand and the soujourn in Mallorca, his sickness and
untimely death, all this seen against the suffering of his
country — — — has set the figures surrounding and preceding him
back further in the shadow. In the same musical current, only the
spectacular Liszt could really stand up as a person against such
competition.

All the same, there seems apparent a wish by later writers, which
was far less evident among earlier, to keep the idol Chopin, the great
original, inviolably so (or as nearly so as possible). Yet while we do
not think less of Bach because of his borrowings and reworkings, it
appears to me that it would not necessarily reduce Chopin's stature
as a composer to find that he did a good deal of the same thing.

Let me say with emphasis that I am a Chopin lover as enthralled
as any, and yet if one is also interested in out of the way or
forgotten music, as I am, a direction in which such a source of
borrowing lies soon becomes apparent. Looking up Field works
(other than the Nocturnes) in the first place for a series of lecture-
recitals on keyboard music, it became clear that what I had read or
been told was a minimal or even non-existent influence on Chopin
became an obviously greater one with each work that I saw. Not in
fact having heard or seen the Irish composer mentioned very much
at all, I had obtained, too, the evidence and conviction of what
appeared to be a by-passed musical connection before I started
looking up in earnest what others had or had not to say about Field
and his influence on Chopin. I found also that earlier writers — — —
who were after all nearer the source — — — made more definite statements as to the existence of this influence than later.

To turn for the moment to what we can find out from writings
on Field (few) as opposed to those on Chopin: *Grove's Dictionary*

does considerably more service in its article on the former (giving less information in that on the latter), where the writer says: "Both as a player and as a composer Chopin, and with him all later pianists and composers who have the least affinity with that master, are much indebted to Field. The form of Chopin's Nocturnes ――― the kind of emotion embodied therein, the type of melody and its graceful embellishments, the peculiar waving accompaniments in widespread chords with their vaguely prolonged sound resting on the pedals ――― all this and more we owe to Field." While the article does not discuss in the same detail Field's more athletic and heroic moods, it states that "In the matter of keyboard technique Field is very much nearer to Chopin than to his master Clementi," and saying that he "must be considered to be very much before his time," it sets out in example the orchestral opening of the second Concerto followed by the piano's first entry.

Heinrich Dessauer, in *John Field, his Life and his Works* (1912), seeing Chopin as Field's "brilliant successor," gives Chopin counterparts to two Field concerto patterns (indicating two more as part of Chopin's musical language) and gives several nocturne reflections, while stressing the nocturne-decorative influence and defining the two 'halves' of the style as Field's the happy and youthful and Chopin's the mature and more melancholic.

Alexandr A. Nikolaev, in *John Field* (Moscow, 1960), according him a wider influence in general and on Chopin, finds the Field-Chopin textural likeness "remarkable" (in melody and accompaniment and many Chopin-design passages in Field concertos and nocturnes) and, if he prints a single Chopin example (a running motif from the first Ballade), gives ample joint-stylistic description.

Chambers Encyclopaedia says of Field: "Among his 16 Nocturnes No. 7 in A and No. 8 in E flat (Liszt Edition) demonstrate well the debt which Chopin owed him;" and the *Encyclopaedia Britannica* gives: "Born 30 years before Chopin, he was one of the earliest of the purely pianoforte virtuosi, and his style and technique strikingly anticipated those of Chopin. This romantic and individual musician was at his best in shorter pieces, where his charming and expressive melodies and his imaginative harmonies, often effectively chromatic, are not exposed to the strain of long development. Field wrote seven pianoforte concertos and four sonatas, in which high quality is often apparent but not consistently maintained." Here we have a clue to the neglect of Field's larger works (only a little remedied recently), due to which any influence from them has been generally unnoticed and discounted.

David Ewen, in the *Encyclopaedia of Concert Music*, writes:

"Though little known as a composer, and rarely performed, Field holds an important place in the growth and evolution of piano music. He was one of the earliest of the Romantics, whose impact on later piano composers was profound. He both anticipated and influenced Chopin. As Liszt noted, Field's works cleared the way for all subsequent efforts appearing under the names of Songs without Words, impromptus, ballades, and the like." From this and the previous quotations it may be seen that not all modern writers restrict the influence so markedly when writing about Field, though they tend to do so, or to dismiss it, when writing about Chopin. David Ewen, however, while extending (along with Liszt) the scope of the Nocturne to include impromptus, ballades and their like, is basically still concerned with the dreamy Field, and does not comment on any more athletic aspect or influence.

It is the view we get with older writers which most strongly allows this aspect also (though I hope to show that the view could even so be wider still). Perhaps, after so much setting out of opinions, that of the Prince among those writers nearer to Chopin's time, Frederick Niecks, and one other, may suffice. Niecks, in his *Frederick Chopin as a Man and Musician* (1888, two volumes), speaking of the composer's "earlier virtuosic style, of which," he says, "we see almost the last in the concertos," gives as his view: "Indeed, we may say of this style that the germ, and much more than the germ of almost every one of its peculiarities is to be found in the pianoforte works of Hummel and Field, and this statement the concertos of these masters, more especially the former, and their shorter pieces, more especially the nocturnes of the latter, bear out in its entirety. The widespread broken chords, great skips, wreaths of rhythmically measured ornamental notes, simultaneous combinations of unequal numbers of notes (five or seven against four, for instance) etc., are all to be found in the compositions of the two above-named pianists. Chopin's style, then, was it not original?" Niecks concludes that it was, by what was made of the commixture of known elements, "the absolutely new being, generally speaking, insignificant compared with the acquired and evolved." With writers on Chopin of the present day, when a rather different view on stylistic originality is generally held, and in the absence of the bulk of the sources, rather many of these have been pointed to as being his fingerprints and illustrating the newness of his idiom. Niecks speaks elsewhere of Chopin teaching his pupils the Nocturnes and Concertos of Field, and one may notice that while he favours Hummel's Concertos as a source of 'peculiarities' reappearing in the Polish composer's music he does not exclude those of Field.

Charles L. Capon, writing in *Famous Composers and their Works* (Boston, U.S.A., 1891), says of Field in his biographical chapter devoted to that composer: "That more than any pianist he set a direct impress on Chopin's artistic style, is more than implied by letters written by Chopin from Paris and Dresden, in which he refers to Kalkbrenner, Klengel and many others who mentioned the marked similarity of his playing to that of Field;" and again that "In the Field nocturne appeared a new element which was destined to work as unique an innovation as can be cited in the history of pianoforte music." Speaking of Field's Concerto in A flat major (No. 2), Capon says that it "was often played by Chopin," and that its first movement "was undoubtedly made use of by Chopin as a model for his concerto in F minor." These extracts from the writings of these two authors will make it clear that in the nineteenth century we had writers (on Chopin and Field) seeing in Chopin's works a wider Field influence than just that of the Nocturnes.

To return to the statement made by Charles Fox that Chopin "brought an entirely new sound into keyboard music;" this may now be suspected to be less likely to be true. The sound, and a multitude of the ways in which its expression was varied, was in fact John Field's, Chopin's contribution and the reason for the lasting recognition of his music lying in the addition of other factors to it and not primarily in the sound itself, which was not, as many of his admirers have thought, an original element of his invention.

Such a statement needs, of course, supporting with evidence, which in this century, with the bulk of Field's music unavailable, was not possible without considerable research. Indeed, until the *Musica Britannica* volume of the scores of the first three Concertos appeared in 1961, at a price necessarily above most people's reach, only the Nocturnes and the three Sonatas, Op. 1 (which apart from the Rondo of the first show little that is characteristic) were still obtainable. The Nocturnes, while taken as a whole they show the newness of the composer's sonority and his pianistic inventiveness, and while in the best of them Field emerges as a perfect miniaturist, reveal at the same time another aspect, in that by no means all of them are equally confident in the direction of the music. This in turn leads one towards a reason for the lack of frequency in their performance, despite Field's romantic translation in them of opera-like melody and embellishment into terms of the piano and the spell-binding quality of those in which he did achieve a perfect balance of shape and content. Indeed, to those knowing his Nocturnes ——— or one or two of them ——— and not the dates of the two composers, it might seem that Field was the imitator of

Chopin and not the innovator, and I have sometimes had this suggested to me. It might also seem unlikely that Chopin, so perennially performed, could owe something to a composer for so long almost completely shunned.

The truth is that (though the search in it for the seeds of Chopin's style and at the same time the jewels of Field's invention is endlessly fascinating) there were factors in the latter's music which led to its almost entire neglect and unprocurability, until very few people knew what any of it sounded like. And though their numbers will be less now, when we have a few more performances, mostly of some of the Nocturnes, and recordings of a number of these and the first two Concertos (but still only a little has been recorded),* it was not surprising that many musical people had never heard of Field. Of those that had, many knew only of the Nocturnes and that Chopin was said to have taken the title of his from Field's, and not all of those had seen or heard any of the latter's. Hence the extent of his keyboard innovations remained unknown or forgotten, with the bulk of his music in old editions in museums or private collections.

Certainly other influences on Chopin's style are valid: his contrapuntal leanings from Bach as well as perhaps the perpetual motion of most of the Études stemming from Bach's Preludes in the ' Forty-eight ' (the writers of studies like Cramer and Clementi come into this too and, one would think, more so), and his running basses under slower-pacing tunes from Hummel (and Field too), as well as technical devices and moods appearing in a number of Hummel's works but focussed mainly in his Concertos and particularly in his first Concerto in A minor, Op. 85. Sonorities and moods suggesting Chopin appear in works occupying roughly the second half of Hummel's output, whose meeting and friendship with Field in Moscow and his likely awareness of that composer's work before this, coupled with the sudden change from a classical to a romantic bias in his own music, would suggest another possible Field influence. A far greater proportion of Field's music than of Hummel's suggests Chopin (this characteristic flavour being noticeable in the first Nocturnes and the second Concerto of the former), and as it is in the all-important realm of poetic feeling and sonority that we must look for the main key, we are brought back basically to Field.

Here ——— as a final example of a twentieth century writer's guarded admission of influences in Chopin's music ——— is what Paul Henry Lang, in his *Music in Western Civilization,* published in

* Further works recently recorded include Concertos Nos. 3 and 5.

New York in 1941, says of Chopin: "This art is original, independent. There were some germs that came from Beethoven's last sonatas, and more tangible influences from Field, Dussek, Hummel, Kalkbrenner and from the idolized Mozart, but when they were absorbed they became thoroughly original."

"Original" was perhaps not the right word ——— "personal" might have been a better, and I hope we shall be able to see from the ensuing analysis in what way Chopin's music was this and how much a development of Field's innovations in pianistic devices and patterns as well as romantic colouring. When one is able to study the latter's music to any extent, including the Concertos as well as the smaller works, this flavour can strike one forcibly today (and quite apart from the success or balance of the works as wholes), so that the discovery of its varied manifestations becomes continually diverting, and one can imagine the effect it would have on a sensitive composer of the Romantic period such as Chopin.

3.

Field's overwhelming disadvantage, and one which led to the virtual obliteration of his larger works, was the lack of any sure sense of construction. His most nearly satisfactory works of size are the second and seventh[*] Piano Concertos, and these are by no means wholly so, with the seventh, which has the more intricate and, in the first movement, gloomily rich material, being the more rambling in shape. The same lack of direction and balance in shape extends to many of the smaller works, including several of the Nocturnes.

The Concertos bear the look of a large span and are accompanied by full and interestingly laid-out orchestral parts, but on examination of the details prove on the whole to be uncertain in their direction, unenterprising in modulation (and at length) and sometimes so rambling and discursive as to be shapeless, as if the composer were lost in a maze from which he had no idea how to extricate himself. Yet we are continually being faced with his poetic use of the piano, when passages of amazing inventiveness, truly Chopinesque in feeling, will jostle with others of equally extraordinary fumbling, where he will fail to get any melodic or harmonic continuity or growth, and will mark time by such means as interpolated arpeggio passages, or a patchwork made up of bits of themes, or by abrupt closings-down of melodic lines with cadence

* 1st   movement;   the   Rondo   (2nd)   is   far   less   comfortably   shaped.

chords, returning a little later to continue with the material so suddenly quitted. The same uncertainty applies at times to the accompaniment of his melody lines, where he cannot always get apt chords fitted, using for considerable stretches tonic and dominant, and especially dominant seventh; nor can he always solve the major-minor complexion of the melodies themselves, or where accidentals, or tones or semitones, are needed to make these fall naturally on the ear. Or he may return a melody limply to the tonic when it is crying out and has started to go to another key. Yet at other times he will accompany his melodies with the subtlest chromatic harmonies and their complexion and decoration and the sonority and balance of the whole will be exquisite.

Thus in much of Field's music we have priceless jewels in a make-shift setting, and if we want to hear what he contributed in poetic sound we must put up with this, a thing most audiences are unwilling to do. Field, as well as exciting us with a whole new range of sonorities and felicities for the piano, can also exasperate us, not to say bore us, with purposeless rambling. He seems to have lacked the element of self-criticism which would have helped him to pull works taut in shape and encouraged him to rework dull patches and uncomfortable links.

Yet his sense of the orchestra was far greater than Chopin's and in the Concertos both solo and orchestral parts have a real share in the texture, though he will sometimes allow the piano both to state and then embelish a theme, when the first statement would be better played on the orchestra (an aspect of giving too little rest to the soloist which is accentuated in Chopin's works with orchestra). Otherwise Field's orchestra is given plenty to do. It was not the tonal balance but, alas, the direction of the music which needed a more confident shaping. With that, we might have had six more ' key ' romantic concertos instead of a very occasionally revived one, the No. 2 in A flat. No. 1, though it has now had a recording by a foreign company (as has No. 2) owes a good deal to Mozart, with nothing like that master's assurance, and though there are signs in it of Field's awakening to the piano's possibilities, in particular in the arabesques of the slow movement, it is unsure of itself harmonically and reveals little that is completely the composer until its delicate and subtle final page. But it, like the Sonatas, shows that Field, too, had his jumping-off ground ––– in the music of the classical composers.

It is because of this limitation in structural ability that Field, for all his fame and success during his lifetime both as a great performer and as a composer, emerges in rather much of his music as an inspired amateur (or we might put it, an "amateur professional") who, despite his brilliant invention of new sonorities stemming directly from the keyboard of the piano, possessed a limited aptitude for setting these out to the best advantage and seemingly never troubled to strive for the mastery of the craft side of composition as it relates to form.

Certainly Field's pianistic innovations would have had small chance of influencing other composers' styles had his music always been as little known as it is today. But we have no reason to imagine this was so and, while very much less has been written about him than about Chopin, a little reading only of what has been written will convince us that this was not the case. Field was not only greatly admired as a virtuoso ――― the German musicologist, Hugo Riemann, described him in his *Musiklexicon* as "one of most original pianistic phenomena," which we may perhaps take as referring not entirely to his playing ――― but his music was much performed, in many countries.

4.

Orchestral introduction to Field's 2nd Piano Concerto.

It would now seem appropriate to say what is known of Chopin's use of Field's music.

Frederick Niecks states that of all concertos Chopin admired most the No. 2 in A flat of John Field and the E minor of Moscheles, which he played and taught to his pupils. And though it seems established that Chopin made his first appearance in public playing a Concerto by Adalbert Gyrowetz (on February 24th, 1818), it has also been said that he first appeared before an audience in a Field Concerto.[1] Niecks says that Hummel, Field and Moscheles were the pianoforte composers who seem to have given Chopin most satisfaction, Hummel and Field being without doubt the pianists who through the style of their compositions most influenced him; too, that he schooled his pupils most assiduously in the Nocturnes as well as the Concertos of the last-named, who was, in the words of one of these, Madame Camille Dubois, "an author very sympathetic to him." His pupil Mikuli says that he had a predilection for Field's A flat Concerto and the Nocturnes, and that he used to improvise the most charming embellishments to the latter when playing them. But he complained strongly when Liszt did the same to a composition of his, Chopin's, own.

Chopin's French pupil, Georges Mathias, says that he studied with him Clementi, Bach, Field (much being played, notably the Concertos), Beethoven, Weber and others. Madame Dubois gives Clementi, Bach, Hummel (*La Bella Capricciosa,* Op. 55, Concertos in A minor and B minor, *Rondo Brillant mêlé d'un Thème russe,* Op. 98,[2] the Sonata in F sharp minor, Op. 81, and the Septet), Field (several Concertos, including that in E flat ——— question: Nos. 1, 3 or 4 ——— and several Nocturnes), Beethoven (Concertos and Sonatas), Weber, Schubert, a little Mendelssohn and a little Liszt.

Niecks, speaking of Field's playing, mentions that he had "an immense cantabile," and Mikuli, describing Chopin's in almost the same words, says: "The tone which Chopin brought out of the instrument was always, especially in the cantabiles, immense, only Field could perhaps in this respect be compared to him." We can see this aspect pointed to in Field's music, where he will very frequently mark an accompanying figure *p* (or even *pp*) against an *mf* melodic line (sometimes this is *p* against *f*), indicating that the tunes must be sure to sing out.

Chopin, describing his success in Paris, says: "Finished artists take lessons from me and couple my name with that of Field," and mentions in a letter of August 2nd, 1832, the coming to Paris of Field and Moscheles. He had long wanted to hear Field, and only now had the opportunity to do so. Of this visit Niecks says: "Chopin, whose playing had so often been compared to Field's, and who had again and again been called a pupil of his, would naturally take a particular interest in this pianist. Moreover, he esteemed him very highly as a composer." Afterwards Chopin professed himself disappointed, but there seems all the same to have been an outcome

---

[1] *Routledge's Encyclopaedia,* 1934.
[2] For piano and orchestra and also piano solo.

to the hearing, as we shall see later.

Chopin, too, could not have missed hearing works of Field as a boy and youth in Poland. In 1818, in Warsaw, there being a shortage of performances of larger works, one-hundred-and-fifty enthusiastic amateurs combined to form a concert society, and gave weekly concerts which included each time an overture, a symphony and a concerto, an aria and a finale, among the works performed involving the piano being ones by Beethoven, Field, Ries and Dussek.

5.
Cantilena.

It has often been suggested that Chopin's *cantilene* melodies and flowing basses, as in his Nocturnes, stemmed from the Italian operas of Bellini and other composers of the time, an example of the style being the well-known *Casta Diva* aria from Bellini's *Norma*:

There is, though, no reason why this should be so when Field's music already exhibited these characteristics in keyboard form:

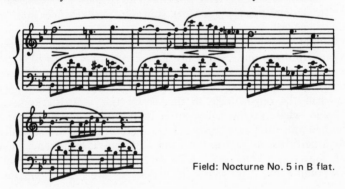

Field: Nocturne No. 5 in B flat.

Thus those holding the former view (as Hubert Foss in his article) overlook, or do not know, that Field had already made this transmutation into terms of the keyboard ――― singing *cantilena* on the piano ――― from the time when in Russia in the early eighteen-hundreds he visited performances of Italian opera, then a fashionable form of entertainment, along with his friends among the nobility and his pupils. (That is, if it was a transmutation and not, at least to some extent, a spontaneous growth, with music taking a more romantic course generally, this linking as far as the keyboard was concerned with the increased expressive possibilities of the piano.) Indeed, would it not be more likely that Chopin absorbed the style from Field, whose music he played, and if there was to be a transmuter of it into keyboard terms that it was Field, who was the first on the scene, and not Chopin? Historically, Field has far better credentials to be Chopin's source, since Donizetti's first opera was not produced, in Italy, till 1818, and Bellini's first, similarly in Italy, till 1825, whereas Field's first three Nocturnes were published in 1814, the Irish composer thus exhibiting the type of melody, embellish-ment and flowing bass before either Donizetti or Bellini did so in operatic terms, and when Chopin was still only four. And this is not all. A portion of the first movement of Field's second Concerto was published in a Russian volume (of piano pieces and songs) in 1811, this movement already displaying the style, in its second subject and a flowing passage in B major in the development section; and as the *Pastorale* of the second *Divertissement* exhibited the style also, this work being published in 1811, Field's known use of this manner is taken back a further three years still. To go forward again, most of the Nocturnes and six of the seven Concertos with, from the second Concerto onwards, their similar use of embellished and *cantilene* melodies, were in print before Bellini's first opera was heard, and also, up to and including the fifth Concerto, before Donizetti's first.

If Field were to be adaptor and not originator it would be from earlier opera composers, and here Alfred Einstein, in *A Short History of Music,* says of Chopin: "In his melody he rescued the charm and sweetness of the best side of Rossini's melody style." ――― which for the same reasons brings us again to Field. Einstein mentions no other influence on Chopin's style and, as has been said, refers to Field nowhere in the book, due, it might be, to the lost music and through this to no thought that he could have had a place in music's development, not even as regards the pianoforte.

Rossini is a more likely candidate. He was born ten years after Field, and his first opera was produced in Bologna in 1810. His *cantilene* melodies were less rich than those of Donizetti and Bellini, and also of Field, but are more florid than those of his two successors:

Rossini: *La Cenerentola.*

Field would thus have had four years in which to have heard Rossini's earlier operas and made a translation of some of their aspects into pianistic terms in the first Nocturnes, but only one or less to achieve the same in the second Concerto's first movement and the *Pastorale* of the second *Divertissement*. Nevertheless, this last linking-up might have been just possible. Again, Field's light-hearted and, on the piano, rather 'tinkling' use of skipped rhythms could have come from Rossini (though not in respect of the Rondo of the first Sonata, published in 1801), that composer working this pattern to death. Also in the operas there appears from time to time what might be described as Field's 'chiming' motif: tonic, mediant, tonic ——— it is evident in the orchestra just before the voice enters in the excerpt given. Field could also have heard, and no doubt did, pre-Rossini Italian opera* in those early years in Russia, to which the excitement created by that composer's stage works would have provided a rememberable climax.

We have thus a far more likely linking: Rossini-Field and Field-Chopin, with the Field-Chopin link more definite than the Rossini-Field. Moreover, Field was already well-known from France to Russia in the early nineteenth century, being taken as we have seen by his teacher, Clementi, to Paris in 1802, where he made an immediate sensation as a pianist, and was thus established as a

---

* e.g. the operas of Vicente Martín y Soler, Spanish composer in the Italian style, who settled in St. Petersburg in 1788, dying there in 1806.

virtuoso in what was later to become Chopin's own territory.

The foregoing conclusion will not, of course, be one to please Chopin isolationists, or those who would like him kept as free from influences as possible, particularly influences from other keyboard. writers, but is the far more likely assumption on the facts available.

It would seem the place to comment here that Gerald Abraham, while he considers "that Chopin's melody is heavily indebted to Bellini's is a commonplace of criticism," sees the debt not to be to Bellini alone, but also to Italian opera in general, and to that extent upholds this view. He finds the evidence of vocal coloratura perceptible in Field also, while not seeming to suspect that Chopin might have obtained this influence from that composer's works, though he says elsewhere that "Chopin learned from Field everything the latter had to teach." Perhaps he does not find this particular factor noticeable enough in Field's music to consider it one which he might have passed on. (The unavailability in print of so many of Field's works, and the fact that the bulk of them would have to be searched out, could partly account for this, though the *cantilena* in the Nocturnes cannot easily be missed, if these pieces as a whole have a cooler complexion than Chopin's of the same title. To see just how much Chopin could and clearly did absorb from Field one needs to know the latter's works more extensively, if possible in their entirety, but at least some of the larger, and one must say that writers in dismissing an influence or allowing a limited one do not seem to have been very concerned to seek out and examine some of these unfamiliar ones.)

Abraham sees Chopin's debt to Hummel to be much greater than to Field ――― technically, that is, to that composer, finding his debt to him to be greater in this respect than melodically, "Chopin's nocturne-type of melody, which is vocal in essence, originating in a very different type of music from Hummel's: Italian opera in general and Bellini's in particular."

Almost, if not quite, alone among writers on Chopin, Arthur Hedley discounts the Bellini influence on the grounds that Chopin had been writing Italianate melodies with similar decorative elements before he had any opportunity to hear an opera by Bellini, and before he formed a friendship with the composer in 1833. (This view receives support from Arthur Hutchings in Alan Walker's book.) Hedley replaces the Bellini theory with an indebtedness to Italian opera in general. But while he concedes that Chopin took the title of Nocturne and its basis of a free form from Field, he does not notice any connection between Chopin's *cantilena* and the fact that Field had written in this style by 1814, when his first Nocturnes were published, and even earlier in the *Pastorale* of the second *Divertissement* and the at least partly written first movement of the second Concerto. The serenity of Field's line in the first Nocturne, which is all the same not without its more plaintive moments, contrasts strongly with the anguished melancholy of the second. Chopin's Nocturne in C sharp minor of 1830, *Lento con gran espressione* (the third of his early, posthumously published ones, the others being the earliest in C minor, date of composition unknown, and the E minor, 1827), is no more pathetic than Field's second in C minor, which sings out its nightingale-heart in entirely ' Chopin' terms, and which can be set against any of the latter's works in similar vein without losing any of its potency.

It is interesting as well as revealing to note that Harold C. Schonberg, in *The Great Pianists,* has these things to say regarding the aspect of *cantilena* in both Field and Chopin. First on Field: "Field's Nocturnes, with their arpeggiated left-hand figurations and Bellini-type melodies, directly inspired the Chopin Nocturnes." And on Chopin: "Chopin adored good singing all his life, was a friend of Bellini, and in his nocturnes tried to capture a Bellinian type of melody over a John Field bass." Why, one wonders, only the bass, when Field had already produced both bass and melody? And why only the Nocturnes? The explanation there is, of course, that the rest of Field must have been to Schonberg, as to others, missing music. Schonberg has clearly seen a similarity in the *cantilena* in both composers' Nocturnes by making the dual comparison with Bellini, and noted a Field-Chopin influence in his remark on Field, half-unsaying this in his remark on Chopin. Both Chopin and Field are thus spoken of as writing melodies like Bellini's ––– and the description is apt in the cases of both these composers. Yet, as we have seen, the bulk of Field's output was published before an opera by either Donizetti or Bellini was produced.

As the dates stand, could not Bellini himself have learned from Rossini, Donizetti and Field (the latter being the earliest born of the three by ten years), or was Italian music so self-contained that it only spread its influence outwards, and received none?

I propose in the following sections to examine in turn Field's Nocturnes, Concertos, and other works, along with the reflections from them ––– in technical devices, melody and embellishments, note- and rhythmic-patterns, basses, and moods ––– to be found in the works of Chopin.

6.
Nocturnes.

Those of the opinion that Chopin merely borrowed the title of
Nocturne from Field cannot, one feels, know the latter's Nocturnes
more than superficially. True, the Field pieces have some diversity,
and not all exhibit to the same extent his romantically inventive
keyboard manner. Several have, at least in part, a more classical bias,
showing in their turn the composer's own musical links.

But the very first two are in Field's special and Chopinesque
manner, and once his Nocturnes begin to lie under the fingers the
wealth they contain of Chopin implications, in melody, basses,
embellishments and moods, becomes increasingly apparent. Whether
due to lack of knowledge, or an urge even to overlook them (which
the gentler flavour of a good many of them helps), it is all the same
strange that in them the fingerprints which are Chopin's and were
Field's before him have not been more clearly remarked, since they,
unlike Field's larger works, have still been available.

Thus Arthur Hedley, while conceding that Chopin took the title
of Nocturne from Field, but otherwise considering his influence to
amount to very little, gives as a Chopin melodic-fingerprint a phrase
which falls and then rises again:

Prelude Op. 28, No. 15.

and

Nocturne Op. 28, No. 2.

not having seen that this is also a Field fingerprint:

Nocturne No. 1 in E flat.

in the second and third bars in the foregoing; and:

Nocturne No. 10 in E minor.

This single facet would not be remarkable did the similarities stop there. But they do not. And to give another joint fingerprint, shared by a Field and a Chopin Nocturne, the former's No. 1 ends with:

and the latter's No. 2 with:

where not only the descending passage but the chiming close in each, and the pairing of the two, are remarkably alike. Field used similar passages again elsewhere, e.g. also in juxtaposition at the end of the nocturne-like slow movement of the second Concerto (this example will be given later), and that movement is based on the chiming motif, which Chopin also uses elsewhere.

In the same Nocturne, Field ends two adjacent phrases with first:

a noticeable anticipation of Chopin's following of:

in the Étude Op. 25, No. 1, the leap of a ninth in the final example, which so tellingly overplays the shorter leap of a sixth in the previous, having often been cited as a particular instance of the later composer's poetic thought. As one plays Field's bars Chopin's come inevitably to mind. Field's leaps are a minor seventh and then that essential and poetic ninth, and his Nocturne was published at least eighteen years before the Chopin Étude was written, the second set of Etudes being composed during the years 1832-36.

To any peruser of Field's Nocturnes one of the most striking examples, and an immediately obvious one, of Chopin drawing upon Field must be that provided by the latter's No. 9 (where again the theme has the falling and then rising fingerprint):

with its close reflection in Chopin's No. 2:

which seems woven from the fabric of the former coupled with the ending of Field's No. 1 (as shown in the preceding examples), and is in the same key as both, E flat. Field's patterns, we shall find, often come out under Chopin's fingers in the same keys, and he will, too, start a Field-derived melody on the same note in the same key (as here, apart from the up-beat), and the chord sequence will at times follow the same track or the same main outline. It may be noted, too, that Chopin has the turn in exactly the same place as Field, between the 5th and 6th three-quaver measures of the bass. This bass was, like Field's more flowing nocturne basses, absorbed by Chopin, who was still using it in his later works, e.g. the 4th Ballade, where it appears as the first reversing and the second according with Field's original disposition of the pairs of chords. It is there too in the climax of the Barcarole.

The theme phrase (in its slightly embellished second appearance) of Field's fifth Nocturne was seen in the section on *Cantilena*. Occurring in this Nocturne, the device of a decorative pattern repeated an octave higher:

is one which Chopin in his turn uses in his Nocturne Op. 32, No. 1:

and the same Field Nocturne contains a pulsing chord passage:

which finds a reflection in Chopin's Op. 32, No. 2, in A flat:

The correspondences here in ideas and feeling for the keyboard will be obvious. Chopin is to be found using the 'method' of the pulsing chords again in the Prelude No. 17 in A flat and towards the end of the A flat Ballade.

Another decorative motif, from Field's Nocturne No. 17 in E:

is reflected in this manner in Chopin's Rondo in E flat, Op. 16:

Field, too, will make use of a device in which a melody is played under a repeated over-note, as in his Nocturne No. 2:

and his Nocturne No. 9:

The same device is frequently used by Chopin, as in his Nocturne Op. 32, No. 1:

Field's second Nocturne makes play, too, with this short motif, which depends for its effect on the repeated note at the end:

He also writes this as ♫♩ with a dotted second note. This triplet based pattern has an equivalent in one which appears in Chopin's posthumous Nocturne in C sharp minor:

It is to be found also in his Nocturne in B major, Op. 9, No. 3, and in the Nocturne in A flat, Op. 32, No. 2 (with the dotted second note), in the Nocturnes Op. 55, No. 2, and Op. 62, No. 1 (in both of these with the ♪ rest), and in the second subject and its ' tail ' passages in the first movement of the B minor Sonata, where it appears as both a plain triplet and with the dotted note.

Field, in his second Nocturne, uses it to introduce phrases, while Chopin uses it sometimes to end them and at others within them. Field in other works uses it in different positions in a phrase and, as Chopin, sometimes in pairs, a second motif beginning on and following from the note on which the first finishes, giving thus a repeated note in the middle and at the end. He also uses it, like Chopin in the last example, as a plain triplet, without the rest or dotted note.

A peculiarly personal facet of Chopin's style is considered to be his melancholy, and though Field exhibits this aspect less often than Chopin, he is by no means without it. Indeed, it made its first appearance as a noticeably individual colouring in his music (the pathos of the second Nocturne was mentioned in the last section), and if we wish to find the bubbling springs of Chopin's nostalgia and brooding, surely they are here in these passages:

Field: Nocturne No. 2 in C minor.

and

Nocturne No. 11 in E flat.

Again, the E minor Nocturne, No. 10, is set in the same nostalgic mood, a typical passage being:

And if we look back at the passage in the Introduction (from the Romance version of Nocturne No. 2) we see again not only this aspect of melancholy and typically Chopinesque filagree, but this striking technical device in the seventh bar:

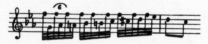

which Chopin made use of later in the Berceuse, in this manner:

and in this:

Indeed, the whole Field passage breathes Chopin.

It is possible to go through Field's Nocturnes one by one and find in each germs that contributed to Chopin's style. Indeed, it is not possible to go through them and, if ones eyes are at all open, miss these germs. Having exampled some of the immediately striking elements and patterns from them, with reflections in the works of the later composer, to proceed now to examine in numerical order those not so far touched on, starting with the third:

The opening of Field's Nocturne No. 3 in A flat:

would seem with little doubt to have had a say in forming the theme of Chopin's Etude in E flat, Op. 10, No. 11, which restates the same (dual) line in chordal terms:

Indeed, if in Field's first bar we link the left-hand's recurring E flat to the right-hand's C and A flat on the first beat and do the same with each subsequent semiquaver half-beat, playing through the bar in chords, we have the right-hand part of Chopin's first two bars in the key of A flat instead of E flat major. Furthermore, the basis of the study would appear to be a combination of the initial melody-line and its under-harmonies of this Nocturne and the continuous left-hand chords (with a comparable melody conveyed by their top notes) of Field's Nocturne No. 7 in C, which we shall come to shortly.

The third Nocturne contains again Field's chiming motif, used at sentence-ends, and the suspended resolution of the close contains a Chopin implication in its outlay and sonority:

with two more bars of dominant seventh harmony in a phrase rising and then falling through two octaves.

——— one can hear just here an approach to the manner of the A flat

Impromptu, which closes like the Nocturne with three A flat chords with the mediant uppermost, Field's top note of these being middle C and Chopin's the C above.

The opening of the Nocturne No. 4 in A (probably Field's most perfect) needs quoting for its Chopin implications. Note the wide-spread, flowing bass and the characteristic sonority (of both Field and Chopin), and the melody which falls and rises, and again falls and rises.

At the double bar Field turns this into a plaintive A minor — — — giving us the tears behind the smiles.

A further bar asks to be quoted, containing as it does a striking example of one of Field's free arabesques. Unevenly matched between the hands, there are thirty-two notes in the right hand against ten semiquavers, or two and a half beats, in the left. All players of Chopin know how frequently he varies and enriches his text with similar arabesques.

A small 'surprise' motif which would appear to have lodged in Chopin's memory is the following:

 Taking a calmer line into a sudden upward flight

in the same way, he gives us this in the Rondo in C major, Op. 73:

This example is from the original solo version of the Rondo; in the second version for two pianos the semiquaver/demi-semiquaver line is given in the first piano part to both hands, which play it an octave apart.

The theme of Field's Nocturne No. 5 is given in the section on *Cantilena*, and patterns from it are among the foregoing examples in this section. This Nocturne, in B flat, is unmistakably and completely Chopinesque in feeling and technical presentation, and should be looked at entire for its pre-creation of a style and mood which have been regarded as exclusively the later composer's. At the time it was published, in Russia in 1816-17 and in Germany in 1817, Chopin could have been no more than seven, and possibly only six.

The sixth Nocturne is the same as the slow movement of the sixth Concerto, with the key changed from E major to F. In $\frac{6}{8}$ time, over a flowing bass, its filagree decorative passages and cadenzas, and a phrase such as the following, which is the embellished restatement at the ninth bar of the opening thematic element of

unmistakably foreshadow Chopin, and this phrase finds a reflection in the fourth bar of his second Nocturne, as:

Field's Nocturne No. 7 in C consists of a continuous melodic line which is formed from the top notes of chords in the left hand ———— chords sometimes wide-spread and arpeggiated, and which only occasionally become single notes or pairs of notes. In the Nocturne's one hundred bars, only six times does the melody line rise into the right hand: for three notes three times, for six notes twice, and for seven notes once.

and

The right hand accompanies with first:

(there being two bars of this pattern before the left hand enters) and then, beginning in the tenth bar, with the following amplification of it:

A more extended version, but what would seem to be a clearly derived one, of this device of a melody resting on spread chords, is evident in Chopin's Etude Op. 10, No. 11, in E flat. The time signature is the same, $\frac{3}{4}$, and when one first plays the Field Nocturne one wonders where one has heard something like it before. The answer is not long to come: in the Chopin Study, which, as has already been said, combines the aspect of the spread chords with the dual theme line of the opening of Field's Nocturne No. 3.

Field's Nocturne in A, No. 8 (in Peters Edition, their numbering being used in this analysis), is a shortened version of the *Pastorale* from the *Divertissement* with String Quartet No. 2, this time for piano alone. The *Divertissement* was published in Russia in 1811, in England in 1811-12, and in France in 1812, and the shortened *Pastorale* was first printed as No. 1 of the *Three Romances* in 1814.

In this Nocturne a simpler version of the bass Field uses in the E flat Nocturne, No. 9, can be seen:

and a typical decorative passage is:

Again I give in the last example the thematic element of

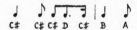

as it is embellished at the start of the subject's second sentence, there being an introductory sixteen bars before the theme appears. The falling chromatic phrase-ending of three notes is one characteristic of Field, and it again reappears under Chopin's fingers, as in these two examples from his Nocturne in E flat, Op 55, No. 2:

and

With its earlier printing as part of the *Three Romances* (and prior to that, before it was shortened, as part of the second *Divertissement*), this eighth Nocturne was probably the earliest written of Field's pieces in the style ——— here we must exclude the *Midi Rondo,* often wrongly included among the Nocturnes, which with String Quartet accompaniment was published as the *Divertissement* No. 1 in or about 1810.

The opening of Nocturne No. 9 in E flat has been seen earlier in this section, where its Chopin links, particularly with his second Nocturne, were shown. As may then have been noticed, its melodic line begins by falling and then rising.

The theme of Nocturne No. 10 has already been given to illustrate this same joint fingerprint of the two composers, which is shown also in the melody of No. 11, and from each piece passages exhibiting Field's aspect of melancholy have been exampled. No. 10 is a delicate, nostalgic and at the same time elegant little poem, which would seem without doubt to have contributed to the forming of Chopin's posthumous Nocturne in the same key of E minor. No. 11 has an extremely subtle opening in an accompanying figure which unfolds in the left hand from a repeated single note, B flat:

and which rises by semitones to the point at which the theme, introduced by three repeated B flats in the right hand, begins at the *mf*:

The Nocturne, though not one of Field's most confident in form, has an extraordinary limpid and floating quality, sensitive melodic variation (all the decorative passages being entirely functional), and uses the upper octaves of the piano to great effect. One can imagine how its whole mood would delight and be sympathetic to Chopin. Here is one of the subtle melodic curves, linking in this case the first and second sentences of the theme:

while the following modulation is one that particularly suggests Chopin:

Chopin uses a variant of this same modulation in his first Nocturne, in the same place on the keyboard, the right hand making use of the same notes:

He bases the close of this Nocturne on this modulation repeated and extended for four bars before resolving in B flat major for the two final bars.

While noting the above similarity, it needs to be said here that this Nocturne was a late Field publication, in 1833, whereas the Chopin B flat minor Nocturne was published in 1832. Thus we are entitled to note the stylistic correspondence but not to conclude the detailed reflection ——— unless it might be a reverse one, or unless the Field Nocturne may like No. 12 have been written well before its date of printing and, considering Field's renown, have been circulated among other musicians in manuscript.

If less extended than the beautiful No. 4 in A major, Nocturne No. 12 in G is uncontrovertibly one of Field's most perfect, and like several of the others it had another source. This Nocturne, which is the slow interlude from the first movement of the seventh Concerto, shows particular Chopin foreshadowings. Here is the theme with its harp-like accompaniment in the left hand:

and here, imperatively needing to be quoted, the end:

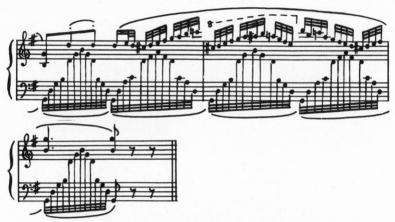

Chopin heard Field play this Concerto in Paris in 1833, and there is reason for thinking that his hearing of it was not unproductive (that is, if he had not already seen it in a manuscript copy, Field having played the first movement in Moscow in 1822). For in 1835 he played his own Grande Polonaise Brillante with the addition of an Andante Spianato:

and

It would be hard not to see the similarities between the Field interlude (Nocturne) and the Chopin movement, in the harp-like basis, floating theme and filagree decoration common to both. Chopin had mentioned in 1830 in a letter that he intended to write a Grande Polonaise with Orchestra, but not the Andante. One has only to play the concluding three bars of the Field (or the opening three

bars) to hear the mood and texture and spianato motion of the
Chopin. In the same key, the tunes in both begin on the same note.
Chopin decorates his melody with more cadenza-like passages and
the movement is longer, but the derivation is obvious.

This Nocturne exhibits another Field device, that of a melody
line implicit in a swifter, undulating technical pattern (the asterisked
notes in the following indicate the melody):

Here is Chopin's use of the same device in the fourth Ballade:

and again in the Fantasie-Impromptu:

Finally, from the same Nocturne, a phrase of Field's nostalgic
melancholy:

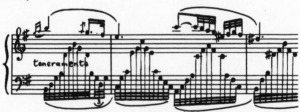

Chopin met Field only once, on this occasion when he heard him
play, and here would seem the place to say that an influence such as
we are discussing could not be expected to come merely through a
meeting, but as such influences do, through an intimate knowledge
of the music lying under the fingers. And this Chopin had. The
writer, for example, acknowledges an influence from French
composers, especially Fauré and Debussy, whom he had no chance
of meeting. Again it was the music itself which provided the
influence.

The Nocturne No. 13 in D minor again exhibits Field's plaintive mood. Another subtle and delicate small poem, it creates a marked effect with quite simple means:

Besides the nostalgic flavour, the melody-line shows again the Field-Chopin fingerprint of falling and then rising. A brighter middle section in the major follows on the first part, before the music returns to the minor and the brooding atmosphere, in which the Nocturne ends.

Field's Nocturne No. 14 in C begins in this manner:

a precedent being provided here for both the basis and the thematic motif of a Chopin piece. The dual use of a pulsing chordal bass and the figure of two notes a semitone apart on the first and fourth beats of the bar in the latter's fourth Prelude constitute what is indeed a close reflection, Chopin merely making his two notes fall instead of rise:

Field's Nocturnes Nos. 13, 14 and 15 are again late publications, No. 14 being written in 1835 and published, with some alterations, in 1836. No. 13 was published in 1834 and No. 15 in 1836. Chopin's Preludes came out in 1839, being written between 1836 and that year.

The main theme and its accompaniment in Nocturne No. 14, and also the theme and accompaniment in No. 15, exhibit somewhat the

mood and manner of Chopin's Rondo in C major (his second version
of which was the Rondo for two pianos). The Chopin, though,
besides being a piece on a much larger scale, was written before the
Nocturnes, in 1828, and of the two latter the second is a lot slighter.
The manner, however, was not new to Field, being employed by him
earlier in the Concertos, in particular the two in C major, Nos. 5 and
6, which were published in 1818 and 1820 respectively. As well as
the similarity in style, these have an abundance of passage-work,
containing patterns which anticipate Chopin's in the Rondo.

Here are the themes of the two Nocturnes, and that of the Rondo
for comparison:

Field, Nocturne No. 14.

Field, Nocturne No. 15 in C.

Chopin, Rondo in C, Op. 73.

A section in the middle of Nocturne No. 14, of a theme in double (and occasionally treble) notes above a widespread. undulating bass, would at first appear to be one with a strong reflection in the middle section of Chopin's first Nocturne ——— this also having a theme in double (and occasionally treble) notes above (for most of its course) the same bass pattern ——— were it not that the Chopin was written before the Field. Field was reported to be distressed by the success of Chopin's Nocturnes to the neglect of his own (six of Chopin's being in print by 1834, with the next two coming out in 1836), and it is possible either that this passage shows a reverse reflection, or points merely to the similarity between the styles of the two composers. If only for the latter reason, a few bars from each piece are worth giving. Field begins his section thus:

the right hand's second phrase is interestingly varied, and contains the characteristic fall of two semitones:

and Field makes the return to the opening motif of the Nocturne in this manner in the bass alone:

Chopin begins his section as follows:

later varying the right hand line by using thirds, fifths and sixths in place of octaves and, having slightly altered his bass pattern in the section's fortieth bar, returns to his first theme in this manner ——— like Field in the bass alone:

Nocturne No. 16 is one of Field's simplest in texture, but exhibits unmistakably his singing of *cantilena* on the piano. The main theme (which appears after sixteen bars introduction) and its accompaniment could have come from an opera of Rossini, Donizetti or Bellini, particularly the last two composers, but has to be recognised as truly Fieldian:

This Nocturne, published in this form in 1836, was originally written as a Quintet for Piano and Strings.

Nocturne No. 17 in E is a solo version of the *Grande Pastorale* for Piano and String Quartet, which was published in England in 1832 and France in 1833. In Liszt's edition of the Nocturnes the introductory section is missing and the middle part shortened. Field made a much shorter solo version which was never published. The longer form of the Nocturne, and the one contained in most of today's editions, is without question the most satisfactory, hanging together unexpectedly well for one of Field's more extended pieces. After an introductory section of thirty-four bars, this theme appears:

Evident again are the bass Field used in Nocturnes Nos. 8 and 9 (and Chopin in his second Nocturne and fourth Ballade) and an opera-like melody presented by Field in terms of the piano.

In the centre of the Nocturne he turns this melody into the minor, and returns to give it in the major in the bass, with a filagree right hand pattern in demi-semiquavers above it:

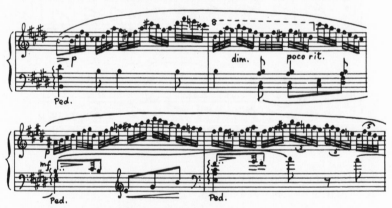

the right hand pattern becoming after a further two bars an embellished version of the melody-line:

One wonders who indeed would not hear Chopin in these bars ----
for instance, his use of the running right hand in the F sharp
Impromptu, a technical decorative pattern that still preserves
melodic subtlety, as it does also in Field's hands. The rocking left
hand B which leads into the theme might, too, be noticed, Chopin
having used this same rhythm on a repeated note to open the second
Ballade. Field uses this same device again with even closer similarity
in an interlude in the last movement of the fifth Concerto, where the
whole section, like the opening one of the Ballade, is based on
rocking chords in $\frac{6}{8}$, which have first a gently lilting melody and
then filagree but melodic semi-quaver figuration as a top line.

A good deal of the last page and a half of this seventeenth
Nocturne consists of right hand arabesques in demi-semiquavers
which, as such passages do in Chopin's music, still remain melodic
and functional. This same manner of elegant fastidiousness in
passage-work is shared by both composers.

The quoting of the next two examples from this Nocturne seems
essential. In the first Field creates a decorative running passage
round the shape of the arpeggio (in this case two arpeggios in turn),
by using notes adjacent to the notes of the chord, and giving a series
of tiny resolutions on to these notes:

Note especially the rising line, where he writes the semitone below
the chord note and then the chord note itself, and so on up through
the arpeggio. A scale passage would have covered the span, but
would have had nothing like the same effect.

Here is Chopin using the same device in the Polonaise in F sharp
minor, Op. 44:

and also in the Barcarole, where he uses the semitone rising to the chord note in both the downward and upward figures:

Secondly, this bar with its repeated figure of four notes precedes the final running passage which descends from the top E of the keyboard to the bottom E:

Chopin makes use of the same figure in the same key at the lower end of the keyboard to form the basis of the middle section of the Polonaise in A flat, Op. 53, beginning:

The *Midi* Rondo, often included among the Nocturnes (in Peters Edition it is No. 18), being not a Nocturne but a piece in a different style, is discussed in the final section dealing with Field's Other Works.

The ending of Chopin's Barcarole would seem to owe something to the rocking passage which begins the extended coda of this Nocturne (I take out its under melodic part):

in conjunction with the ensuing demi-semiquaver passage-work for the right hand; Field's coda, like Chopin's, ends in a not quite simple scale falling through six octaves (its beginning can be seen at the end of the previous example), which he follows with two E major chords, while Chopin ends his coda with two declamatory pairs of octaves: dominant, tonic; dominant, tonic.

There is another Nocturne, *The Troubadour,* not among the present published ones, its introduction and ending (the latter an octave lower) exhibiting Field's chiming motif:

The theme and manner of the Nocturne would at first seem not very characteristic ——— serenade- rather than nocturne-like and a little obvious to our ears today:

though the subject shows the falling and rising fingerprint and the piece presents at times some chromaticism and subtletly in the chord pregressions. There is, however, a precedent, Field using the same method, of a theme over a pulsing accompaniment in quavers with a rest under each melody note, in the orchestra (but not in the piano) in the first movement of the sixth Concerto (in that case in $\frac{4}{4}$ time), and it is possible the Nocturne was written about the same time. This piece, left out of the subsequent volumes of collected Nocturnes (probably on account of its generally simpler style), was published in England about 1832. To this description one can add that this rather odd little piece has a firm structure and, despite its ingenuous manner, can sound quite pleasant in the playing.

Cecil Hopkinson, in his *A Bibliographic Thematic Catalogue of the Works of John Field*, lists another Nocturne in B flat, published in a Russian musical magazine, and a further, "*Dernière Pensée*," as being mentioned by various writers, but of which there is no record.

The opening of the former, which again has a melody-line which falls and then rises, shows Field using an accompaniment to the theme involving a repeated note (F) reminiscent of Chopin's basis for the D flat, 'Raindrops,' Prelude:

though a more striking example of Field's use of this device will be seen when we come to examine his third Concerto. Either of these two Nocturnes might be the one mentioned by Grattan Flood in his short biographical study of Field as having been written in Vienna in 1835.

7.
Concertos.

The Field Concertos were mainly available at the time in two editions: by Breitkopf and Härtel, and in the French edition of Pacini, the Breitkopf editions coming first and the French from a year to several years later. This order was maintained for the first four Concertos until, in the case of the fifth and sixth Concertos, Russian and German editions came out in the same years, 1817 and 1823 respectively, the French edition of the former appearing abut three years later, and of the latter a year later. The seventh Concerto received a printing which included the orchestral parts in Germany only. These editions consisted of a piano part and orchestral parts (in the case of the fifth Concerto a second piano part also), the scores remaining in manuscript, and presumably being on hire in various copies of the originals. Following these initial complete editions came various printings without accompaniment parts of the whole works or separate movements in the same and other countries (most usually Russia and England), these editions varying as to time of appearance from considerably later to quite soon after the first publications. For instance, an English edition of the first Concerto without parts was published in 1817. In the full scores Field wrote a version of the *tuttis* into the piano parts (often with different harmonies), making these parts continuous throughout ――― an exercise either directed towards the preparation of the piano copies for printing, or more probably since he was in the habit of playing the Concertos, or movements from them, as solos also. This is a method usually adopted with Chopin's Andante Spianato and Grande Polonaise Brillante, which appears to better advantage this way than with orchestra. Breitkopf still had some of the piano parts in print into the 1930s. though one imagines that with the works themselves in disrepute there would not be much interest in what to most musicians would be emasculations of the originals. Thus, with the full scores unobtainable and having to be looked up in libraries, what could have been a fertile area of research, had any the wish to look therein, was cut off. The *Musica Britannica* volume of the scores of the first three (published in 1961) made this position better, but there are still four of the seven Concertos which few have the chance to see.

The first Concerto, in E flat major, contains little that is the characteristically romantic Field, though it has a good many indications of his seeking new means of pianistic expression.

The first subject of the first movement, Mozartian in style,

contains nevertheless (in the seventh bar) a skipped rhythm typical of Field, and later of Chopin:

The following, at the eighth bar after the piano's entry, might be by Beethoven:

until at the sixteenth bar we get a glimpse of Field's more mature manner:

and begin to hear Chopin too, in the type of graceful decorative pattern which adds so much variety to the music of both composers.

An example of Field's seeking new technical devices for the keyboard is the pattern he uses in the second subject:

this later passage from which exhibits rather more colour along with an early example of his marching bass, besides showing the type of modulating progression of which Chopin was later to make such effective use:

Chopin's use of this bass battern will be exampled later.

The slow movement, on a Scottish air, *Within a mile of Edinburgh town,* has a great deal of florid decoration in the solo part, while not being very comfortable harmonically. Field's liking for embellishment was already evident, but his individual use of *cantilena,* waiting no doubt to be sparked off by his hearing of Italian opera in Russia, was yet to come. This Concerto, though not published till 1815, was first performed by Field in London in 1799.

The Scottish theme of the slow movement receives this treatment in the orchestra:

and this in the piano:

where the graceful style of Field's embellishments can be seen and also his use of the higher part of the keyboard. It waits, however, till the coda of the third movement for the fully imaginative and expressive Field to be revealed:

– – – a passage of thirteen bars (before the two final chords) which at the same time conveys a feeling of Chopin in its sonority and the sparkling and yet subtle technical pattern.

Here is Chopin's use of a similar pattern in the E flat Rondo:

also in the Étude in E minor, Op. 25, No. 5:

and in the Berceuse:

The third movement of the Field (of which we have just seen a part of the coda) opens with the following theme:

If we note the tail of the above phrase, marked by the bracket, and then look at the first bar of Chopin's theme in the E flat Rondo, we find that, with the exception of the E flat, he used the same notes describing the same melodic curve, with the difference that he gives the second half of the pattern a skipped rhythm:

In another part of the Rondo Chopin keeps the rhythm even:

This movement also provides a *bravura* pattern used by Chopin at a point of climax in the original solo version of the two-piano Rondo, and in the first piano in the two-piano version, where the second piano has an added semiquaver line in counterpoint in the right hand. Here is the Field:

and two more bars

and here is the Chopin:

and three more bars

The same pattern is to be found in the first movement of Chopin's Concerto No. 1, beginning in the fourth bar after the piano's entry.

Though the Concerto is immature Field, showing less Chopin foreshadowings than his later Concertos, one or two other pointers towards the later composer's style may be noted. The first movement, for instance, reveals a Chopin peculiarity in that Field goes straight from the development into a recapitulation of the second subject, omitting a return of the first subject, as Chopin does in the first movements of the B flat minor and B minor Sonatas. Field's pianistic sonority, too, is admirably transparent, and the Concerto contains a good deal of passage-work with indications of his later manner and what might be described as *pre*-pre-Chopin implications, such as this (in the first movement):

(Concerto No. 2)

The material of the second Concerto (published in 1816) is something quite different, and here we are face to face with Field's mature pianistic inventiveness. Though possessing imperfections (mostly in the shaping) which have led to its neglect in the concert hall, this work remains Field's most considerable achievement, exhibiting all the facets of his style ——— the heroic, the scintillating, the delicate and the expressive. The orchestral opening has already been quoted at the beginning of Section 4. This Concerto is a 'key' romantic one, with probably more influence on later romantic piano writers than any other. Its first movement at least is said to have served Chopin as a model for that of his Concerto No. 2 in F minor (written before his No. 1 in E minor), and the feeling of his style cannot be missed in the theme, and its half-close of:

Chopin's half-close to his theme is:

The piano's entry needs quoting for its Chopin implications:

The Concerto has a large span, if, as has been said, some discomfort in the form, uncertainty in this respect being most noticeable in the last movement. While the first Concerto was mentioned as being an immature work, it is necessary to say that in the structural aspect of his longer movements Field never did reach full maturity. The first movement of this Concerto comes nearer than most to a balanced shape, if it can still not be called completely satisfactory. But the originality of the ideas, in their romantic colouring and pianistic effectiveness, is a different matter.

This Concerto abounds in Chopin-like devices and whole pages could be quoted. The lead-in to the second subject cannot but remind one, like the ending of Field's first Nocturne, of the cadenza passage at the end of Chopin's Nocturne No. 2:

while to go back four-and-a-half bars (that is, to the seventh bar from the end of this passage) we have in the right hand:

the basis of Chopin's 'Minute' Waltz, Op. 64, No. 1, written by him in quavers in quick $\frac{3}{4}$ time, the right hand having the same repeated note-series ——— G natural, A flat, C, B flat ——— two octaves lower, over a waltz bass, the bass chord and the key being now D flat. To give here the first eight bars of Chopin's right hand line:

the bracket contains the repeated figure in question. The bass enters and the theme proper begins at the fifth bar. We shall see later an example of Field using the same figuration in the sixth Concerto.

The simple statement of the movement's second subject makes use again of Field's characteristic skipped rhythm:

Chopin, too, frequently makes use of this rhythm –––– for instance in the F minor Nocturne, Op. 55, No. 1, the opening section of the Fantasie, and the Allegro de Concert.

The immediately following embellished version of this subject is:

Field, however, makes the piano play both the simple and the embellished versions, whereas the former would clearly have been better given to the orchestra. (As in the Chopin Concertos, so in those of Field, the piano, once it has entered, tends to play continuously, or almost so, with few passages, apart from the between-section *tuttis,* given entirely to the orchestra by way of relief. Field's accompanying parts, though, are considerably fuller and more imaginative than Chopin's.) But, while the contrast would have been helped by the orchestra taking over the first of these two statements, particularly to be noted, as making its first, fully-expressive appearance in the Concertos, is Field's *cantilena* writing for the solo instrument, shown in the last example and in the extension of the subject which follows it:

which he immediately repeats *pp* in the minor with poignant effect:

The mood changes again with the *bravura* section which ensues, from which this technical pattern for the right hand:

has a near-relation in the following from Chopin's first Ballade, which ——— in its shape, key, repeat, use of the same note-span, and notes except A natural, in the same part of the keyboard ——— would seem only a slightly telescoped version of the former:

Another pattern of a like description contained in the same section (given here as it occurs in A flat major in the recapitulation ——— it is in E flat in the exposition):

compared with the first phrase of Chopin's Mazurka in A flat, Op. 7, No. 4, reveals him using a similar convoluted pattern in the third and fourth bars, in the same key and with the same curl in the tail:

This movement is one of Field's most adventurous in regard to key contrasts. The following is the start of the long *cantilena* melody in B major in the development, the piano playing against low tremolando chords in the strings, with the bassoon adding small melodic counter-statements:

Lovely as it is in idea, and how Chopinesque in feeling, this passage reveals Field's sometime discomfort in the harmonies fitted to his melody-lines, which either do not change where the melody suggests they need to, or if they change do not always do so to accord with its harmonic implications.

An excerpt from the first movement was printed in St. Petersburg in 1911, in a volume of piano music and songs by various composers. This began at the F major statement of the second subject in the development, fifteen bars before the F minor section, of which the following is the beginning,

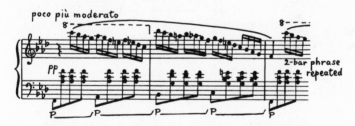

and continued for a further forty-two bars of that section. This printing gives some idea of the time of composition of at least the first movement of the Concerto.

Harold C. Schonberg speaks of Chopin's "functional ornamentation," saying that "unlike so much of the music of Liszt and the other virtuosos, nearly all Chopin's bravura passages ――― and all, in his maturity ――― have a melodic rather than a purely bravura function."

Is not the same true of passages of this type in Field's music which we have so far examined, and in such as the following? ——— again from the F minor section, I quote first the *pp* opening and then the *ff* close of the piano part's final thirteen bars:

In the recapitulation, in the *bravura* section which follows the second subject, another of Field's individual technical patterns appears:

Chopin is to be found using the same descending finger-pattern in the coda of the fourth Ballade (note that, like Field, he writes thirds on the second and third semiquavers of the first three-note pattern, and subsequently a third on the third semiquaver only):

A near variant of this pattern is to be found in the slow movement of Chopin's Concerto No. 2, in the twenty-first bar, the first note of each three-note pattern being placed one degree lower to allow of thirds on the second and third semiquavers throughout.

To leap ahead for a moment to Field's fifth Concerto, in the first movement of that work he uses his pattern in triplets, exactly as Chopin does:

Field's chiming motif appears a good deal in this work ――― here it is as used in the climax of the recapitulation:

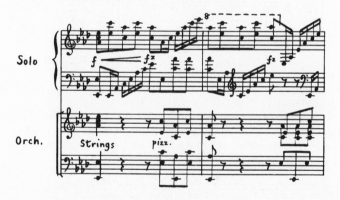

The solo part of this movement ends with a trill in the following form:

while Chopin in the E flat Rondo makes use of this two-bar trill pattern:

The basis of the slow movement is again the chiming motif:

Here is Chopin saying very much the same thing in the second theme of the first Ballade:

The similarity in pace is noticeable, and once more a Field motif has come out under Chopin's fingers in the same key.

Two more excerpts from this movement, which has all the langour and sighs of a Chopin Nocturne, ask to be quoted. This passage with its feeling of climax followed by a quasi-cadenza occurs halfway through the movement:

Again the sonority and delicacy inevitably remind one of Chopin. The device of working up to a climax followed by a cadenza was to become a feature of romantic piano music (Liszt making too constant use of it), and similar instances in Chopin are the endings of his second and third Nocturnes and the passage of four bars, Nos. 57-61, in the Nocturne in B major, Op. 32, No. 1.

The ending exhibits the following filagree rising and falling pattern leading into a final few repetitions of the chiming motif:

Again we are reminded of the endings of Field's Nocturne No. 1 and Chopin's No. 2, the key being the same, E flat, in all three cases.

The third movement contains more than a few Chopin fore-shadowings.

Here is the theme:

which, in the thirty bars that follow, Field embellishes with semi-quaver patterns, simple and in triplets, and short cadenzas.

The contrasting passage which ensues in the orchestra (after sixteen bars the piano adds a decorative semiquaver running line for a further seven) is based on this motif:

Comparing the orchestral passage in the same place in the third movement of Chopin's E minor Concerto, we find that he begins it thus:

Soon we have Field in full flood of chromatic and decorative piano writing ——— the type of melodic *bravura* passage previously referred to, such as:

and

The similarity between the last passage and that leading into the second subject in the exposition of the first movement of Chopin's Concerto No. 2 will be obvious to anyone who plays over the two passages, in the Chopin from:

through:

In the latter example may be seen a repeated chromatic figure noticeably similar to that in bars 4, 5 and 6 in the Field excerpt (though an octave lower, it spans the same notes, G to the F above) along with a reflection of Field's bass pattern, with the dominant played not on a main beat, but after ––– chord up, dominant down, each time.

This in the Field:

would seem to be paraphrased by this in the slow movement of Chopin's Concerto No. 2:

Field's movement contains a middle section which opens with a more tranquil theme given to the strings, to which the piano adds a graceful, almost musical-box-like obligato:

In the theme itself, with its gently marching character (later growing stronger) we see a definite element in Field's style. The second subject of the first movement of this Concerto is of the same nature, and we shall see the same element again later. To the Chopin enthusiast it will not need pointing out that this type of theme is a feature in his style also, examples being found in the C minor Funeral March (particularly the A flat theme), in the Fantasie, the Allegro de Concert and the F sharp major Impromptu (the D major theme). In Field's middle section the piano finally shares in the tune-line, which leads into a development of the first orchestral episode, taken at half pace against a running accompaniment:

before the return is made to the opening (rondo) theme in what is to be its last appearance.

In this development another joint facet in the styles of both composers begins to emerge. A marked feature in Chopin's music is his use of running basses, which provide a decorative line in the left hand in counterpoint to a melody line in the right. Mozart used this bass in a somewhat simpler form, usually as a method of response, by reversing the roles of the hands in a just-played phrase to which he had given a bustling right hand and a simpler left. The employment of this bass is, however, more marked in Field, who uses it in the way Chopin does, by giving the left hand the decorative role by intention and not through a formal reversal, and the latter part of this movement sees him making effective use of it. Twice in the extended passage under discussion Field takes the run over into the right hand, and into the upper part of the piano, while the left hand has the tune-line in the middle of the keyboard, and sometimes he allows the right hand to share in the semiquaver motion in counterpoint to the left hand. The following example occurs during this section:

while this shows Chopin using a bass of the same type in the *Là ci darem* Variations:

After restating it first on woodwind, horns and timpani, Field gives the return of the main theme this treatment in the piano:

while in the Trio in G minor, Op. 8, Chopin gives the piano this pattern to play in the second subject of the first movement:

Leading into the extended coda, Field writes a series of declamatory and chromatic chords which must inevitably remind the hearer of similar passages in Chopin. Coming in under a glittering flight of semiquavers in the solo part, the orchestra starts the passage with three bars of chords in a gradually mounting sequence:

which links directly with this in the piano:

the orchestral line being continued in support of the solo with corresponding chords and the same bass progression in the two octaves below.

For comparison, here is a declamatory chord passage from the Allegro de Concert:

Though the more extreme chromaticism of the last example is obvious (Chopin's passages of the type can all the same vary in that respect), this chromatic element is part of the nature of both series (in the Field from where the piano takes on the line). Also it may be noted how Chopin, like Field, puts his passage together in short melodic sections forming a sequence. Again, in an earlier example in the same piece (from bar 27 to the first three quavers in bar 30), Chopin makes both parts of his phrase, the simpler as well as the more chromatic, follow sequences. The tune-line of the last (simpler) portion of this (bar 29 into bar 30) will illustrate this:

Here it may be objected that these passages in the Allegro were originally for the orchestra, Chopin having at first intended the piece to be the opening movement of another concerto. However, since he uses the same type of passage to lead up to the coda of the F minor Ballade and during the codas of the finales of the B minor Sonata and the F minor Concerto, it is shown to be a definite facet of his

piano style. In this connection, other writers have commented on
the orchestral nature of some of Chopin's keyboard effects, it being
said that he could evoke such effects from the piano in a way that
others, but not he, did from the orchestra. Here, taking the two
Field examples together, we may mark that the piano completes the
line begun by the orchestra (which in fact continues below the
soloist in support), the type of passage thus having in his hands both
an orchestral and a pianistic basis. Field, in the Polacca of the third
Concerto, writes another such declamatory passage (leading to a new
section in the movement), this time for the piano alone. The passage
will be given later, but to quote the tune-line of the first two bars is
apt here, since it contains the melodic curve (also in sequence) which
Chopin is to be seen using in the first example from the Allegro de
Concert:

A feature of Field's style is what might be called his
' epigrammatic ' passages, short episodes of a few bars, more often
than not repeated, which are separate and complete ideas in themselves, based usually on chord sequences which move away from the
tonic and back to it. Here are two of these — — — the first appearing
earlier in the orchestra in a simpler chordal version:

with an answering phrase downwards

Following immediately is this episode, which also shows Field's
marching bass (to be discussed further later):

the phrase repeated with a slight variation

These episodes carry on the music not by development but by a succession of rounded-off ideas, and are a feature of Chopin's style also ――― for instance, following the second subject in the first movement of the B minor Sonata, where the exposition and the recapitulation are each completed by means of four such episodes (two short and two longer) and a tail phrase, with a short *bravura* coda, based on the opening flourish of four semiquavers, added after the recapitulation to bring the movement to a close. An even more noticeable example is provided by the Tarantelle, which is constructed mainly on an episodic basis. While two themes and one episode in the piece reappear, it contains no less than seven other episodes (six of sixteen bars and one of eight), each of which is a separate invention. The squared, sectional aspect is maintained throughout, and only in the last page does any theme or episode show an aspect of change or development within itself. This is not to minimize the vigour and effectiveness of the Tarantelle or the poetry of the Sonata, but to mention a point of style.

The previous episode in the Field leads directly into this passage:

where, especially after the repeated bars,* may be seen a waving figure which gives a strong reminder of Chopin's floating pattern in the A flat Étude, Op. 25, No. 1, which is Field's pattern:

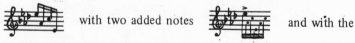

rustling semiquaver motion likewise kept up in the bass in contrary motion. Another example, particularly striking, of Chopin clearly adapting a Field figure by turning a pattern of four notes into one of six, will be seen when we come to the sixth Concerto.

On the debit side, Field's movement possesses a 'spare' thematic motif in A flat minor:

which contributes nothing to the shape or the colour; it receives no development and would be better omitted. Field seems to have written it for want of a better way to introduce the central section in B major, and it then occupies twenty-four bars, being alluded to briefly once later. Had he looked a little further, the perfect solution lay to hand ——— the first phrase of the just-concluded orchestral episode turned into the key of A flat minor (from A flat major) and extended for a bar or two would have effected the link both more economically and more expressively. Structurally, too, Field seems more than once to be trapped in a maze, from which he finds the way out with difficulty. By contrast, there is an abundance of colourful and romantic ideas coupled with a truly original pianistic inventiveness. Surprising as the rondo must have seemed at the time it was written, with a little tightening it would still be irresistible.

(Concerto No. 3)

The first subject of the first movement of the third Concerto, in E flat major, is based on a repeated note in an uneven rhythm:

Again there is the characteristic skipped pattern at the half-close.

The Concerto contains a lot of original and effective piano writing, while a reason for its neglect ——— in structural indetermination ——— is not difficult to see. For instance, the second subject, though it has a certain tenderness, strikes an undecided note by moving, over a few nearly related chords, a little way away from its basic key and returning to it, in nearly every bar. In short phrases, its plaintive aspect holds the attention for a few of these, and then one becomes aware that Field has lost direction and is rather tentatively marking time. In general, the quality of the ideas is vastly

in advance of the shaping of the movements. In this case there are
two movements only, and other writers have suggested that Field
may have been in the habit of playing a Nocturne, without the
orchestra, between them. On the other hand, since the second movement, a Polacca, contains a slower section before the final return of
the main theme and the conclusion, it is just as likely that he may
have intended the Concerto to be played as it is. The seventh
Concerto similarly has only two movements, with a slow interlude in
the middle of the first one.

The Chopin foreshadowings in the work are again considerable.
The piano's statement of the theme starts simply:

but after eight bars there is a sudden flowering into arabesques. The
passage is given here as it occurs at the start of the development
— — — at its first appearance, as part of the theme, it follows on in E
flat major, with less extended bass chords:

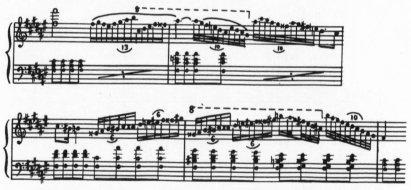

In addition to the melodic-*bravura* complexion of the arabesques,
the pattern of three notes falling by semitones (already noted in the
section on the Nocturnes), characteristic of both Field and Chopin,
can be seen at the beginning of the third bar.

The lead-in to what at first appears to be the piano's second
subject, and this subject itself, would, to those who know nothing of
Field, automatically say "Chopin." This beautiful idea is, however,
not the second subject which was given in the orchestral intro-

duction and which occurs a little later in the piano, but a ' bonus '
theme, which appears only the once. One could call this subject
number 2a, the true second subject being number 2b. After four bars
of modulating chords in the orchestra, the piano enters with:

The subject itself begins at the third bar. Both the Chopinesque
curves and elegance of the whole melodic line can be noted, and also
once more the chromatic fall of three notes in the tail, while here
again is Field singing *cantilena* most persuasively on the piano. We
have, too, a particularly good example of his marching bass, in the
last bar and a half of the above, and in the rounding-off of the
subject, thus:

Here would seem to be the opportunity to enlarge upon this bass,
of which Field makes such noticeable and effective use, by giving
examples of its employment by Chopin, of whose style it is a
distinctive feature also. The latter is to be found using the bass in his
Nocturne in F minor, Op. 55, No. 1, along with the skipped pattern
we have noted occurring at the half-closes of the first two Field
Concertos and the present one:

Chopin uses this bass, too, in the Fantasie — — — in the opening
section:

and in the modulating passage of eight bars beginning:

Other instances are in the Nocturne in C minor, Op. 48, No. 1, and
the Étude in G flat, Op. 25, No. 9.

The second subject proper cannot match the expressiveness of the
preceding G flat major theme, though Field, in transferring it to the
piano, adds embellishment so as to give it more variety than it had in
the orchestra, without being able very successfully to disguise its
essentially static nature, due to too many full-closes in its tonic key
of B flat. Similarly an addiction to too-constant full-cadences
reduces the impact of much of the lavish passage-work in the movement, though the effect can be enchanting when this breaks free.
The second subject, all the same, shows elements, one in particular,
which have reference to Chopin. Here is its opening, there being only
slight differences between these bars as given to the piano and as
heard earlier in the orchestral introduction:

Small in itself, but made more noticeable by being repeated and through the use of the subdominant minor chord, the element spanning the fourth beat of bar 4 to the third beat of bar 6 would seem to have made an impression on Chopin. (Field's repeated element is there in three of the subject's four appearances: in the orchestral introduction, in the piano in the exposition and the development, being omitted in the recapitulation.) In the Introduction to his Rondo in E flat, after two annunciatory phrases of two bars each, Chopin writes the following, beginning on the fourth beat of bar 4:

A matter again of Chopin taking a Field motif a little further? That this is at least likely is encouraged by Chopin's two opening phrases, which have an equivalent squareness and serve the same function of a dual announcement as Field's two, and by the element in question starting in the same place as to beat and bar in both cases. But Chopin, unlike Field, avoids monotony in key and line by giving the skip in his element a melodic shape and then moving first the chords and then the whole motif down the keyboard. He follows a similar procedure with his opening phrase:

by taking its repeat up into F minor, and giving two later repeats of it in B flat and E flat minors respectively.

Of the closeness of the next two examples (the first by Field and the second by Chopin) there can be no question. Field, in giving the second subject to the piano, clearly felt the need for some movement, and, following on directly from the opening quoted, this passage suddenly occurs ——— rather too suddenly, as it makes the static aspect of the remainder more noticeable:

The suggestion of Chopin is, however, there strongly in this solitary bar and three-quarters, and a reflection of it is not far to seek ——— this, in the slow movement of his Concerto No. 1, where the melodic line is reproduced almost exactly, the double note on the last semiquaver in the right hand being there also:

Field's phrase appears three times more, with the shape varied a little each time, in the passage-work which rounds off the exposition; and similarly in the recapitulation, while a more circumscribed version provides the main basis of the running passages which form the greater part of the development:

Thus there is no question as to the figure's prominence in the movement.

Before finishing discussion of the second subject, the delicately chromatic ending asks to be quoted:

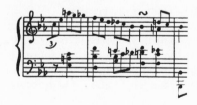

Again Field has been more successful in the invention of small but expressive turns of phrase than in the overall shaping.

Not unlike what were previously described as "epigrammatic" passages in the works of the two composers, Chopin frequently makes use of short modulating passages which move through a number of keys till they arrive again at the starting one ——— a species of chromatic round trip, and a device which gives piquancy to an episode and added interest to whatever theme or idea comes next. Perhaps basically a means of marking time interestingly, the danger of the method is that it can lead to a string of episodes all doing the same thing ——— quitting the main key and coming back to it ——— and in his time Chopin was criticised for his "excessive" modulation, it being said that he ranged through all the keys and if an idea had not turned up by then he finished the piece and left it at that.

We know now that, except in a few plainly novice works, the ideas were always there and always interesting, even in the smallest episode, so interesting as at times to disguise a lack of development ——— though it is not suggested that every work should contain or every composer write closely-argued development after the fashion of Beethoven and Brahms.

The method (of the travelling and returning chromatic passage) was not, however, individual to Chopin, as Field had used it before him, and it is very definitely a fingerprint in the style of both composers.

An example in Chopin is the second of the two quoted from the Fantasie, which ranges from E flat major through G flat, F, A flat, G and B flat majors and then, over a B flat bass note, returns by rising chords of C flat, C, D flat and a dominant seventh chord with augmented fifth to E flat major (8 examples back).

The sixth example quoted from the first Concerto (the one with the marching bass) gives a foretaste of this method in Field, and if his modulation in the example now to be given is not so extensive as that in the Chopin, nevertheless we find him writing the same sort of key-shifting passage in a section which comes after the second subject in both the exposition and the recapitulation. After the constriction evident in the second subject, Field's inventiveness reasserts itself to more continuous effect in an extended floating passage using the upper part of the keyboard. This whole passage has a truly magical quality, with the orchestra accompanying with low chords on the strings over a pizzicato bass and with trills on the woodwind. The passage concludes with these bars of modulation ——— given here from the recapitulation in order to show the more florid decorative figure Field writes in the last bar at the second appearance:

Towards the end of the exposition again, the following two passages, divided by three bars, appear, and bring to mind two of Chopin's technical patterns in the Allegro de Concert, similarly only a few bars apart. The Field patterns are these:

and the Chopin these two:

and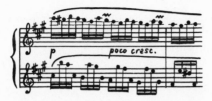

It is of course noticeable that the patterns have added complexity in Chopin's hands. Like Keats building upon the inspiration he received from Barnes, it is as if Chopin, though he had absorbed the earlier composer's style to the pitch of its having become a compelling force, with the constant throwing up of small elements, must nevertheless go one step further. This is how one style develops from another ――― by a process of growth ――― and Chopin's greater complication will be plain in many of the examples presented. This, however, does not disprove the source, and as we know of Chopin's use of the Concerto from his pupils, what conclusion can we draw except that the finger-patterns of the Field went into the shaping of the Chopin? Mere coincidence, in the case of the last two patterns and the convoluted figure from the second subject, and indeed in so many reflections from the same composer, would be unlikely.

We have seen the main basis of the development in the F minor bar quoted. There the piano's entry is led up to by two pensive phrases in the orchestra, the first being of five bars ending in:

Field's second phrase is extended to six bars. In Chopin's Concerto No. 1 the orchestra opens the slow movement with two five-bar phrases, the first ending in:

the second being a restatement of the first in the relative minor with an interrupted cadence on the two crotchets in the fifth bar. Chopin then rounds off the introduction with two bars of sustained chords, the piano entering on the last beat of the second bar. The essential element reflected would seem to be the pattern consisting of the grace-note and the two crotchet chords followed by the minim rest, but it is as if the phrase-span of five bars lingered in Chopin's sub-conscious and had to be reproduced also.

One of the fascinating aspects of going through Field's works is the sudden impressions one receives of particular Chopin pieces. In this movement, in the development, the continuation of the piano's passage-work, after its entry in F minor, contains the following note-patterns: ――― in the right hand:

and in the left hand, against strong right hand chords:

Might these be judged to give a feeling of the mood and particularly part of the *bravura* left hand passage-work of Chopin's ' Revolutionary ' Etude in C minor, Op. 10, No. 12? Let us contrast the following from the Etude and see:

and

There is even an approach to the skipped rhythm Chopin uses in the right hand, in:

During the development the second subject appears in the minor, this convoluted technical pattern leading into it:

Feeling this under the fingers one is conscious of its Chopin affinity, and the mind starts searching for its reflection in his works. It is not long before an answer comes, in the following from the last movement of the Cello and Piano Sonata:

Field's second subject has here more colour than in its other appearances, partly owing to its minor key, and also because he makes a welcome contrast halfway by lifting it into the relative major before moving back into the minor by a series of chromatic chords. The subject has thus more shape than it had initially, with this touch of chromaticism and an attractive melancholy, especially towards the final cadence, giving it a Chopinesque feeling which was only glimpsed before.

The development finishes with a *bravura* climax passage in the solo part beginning:

this being rounded off by an upward C minor arpeggio and four strong crotchet chords. Chopin makes use of the same pattern at a similar point of climax, and if we turn to the piano's final bars in the first movement of his F minor Concerto we find him writing:

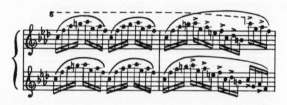

followed by a shake in semiquavers with a conclusion under it in the left hand of likewise four stressed crotchets, these being first a wide dominant seventh chord and then two dominant bass octaves resolving on to the tonic.

The next example, and the last to be quoted from this movement, is given because it shows Field using, as a basis for repetition, a group of notes which overlaps the beat. Thus the accentation, with intriguing effect, falls differently from repeat to repeat:

This device, and not in this case the particular pattern, has its counterparts in Chopin, for instance in the Waltz in F major, Op. 34, No. 3:

If the fifth quoted example in the part discussing the third movement of Field's second Concerto is again looked at it will be seen that the first bars show him using the device there also, in a repeated pattern of six semiquavers spanning a beat and a half with the accentation changing.

The second movement of this Concerto, marked *Tempo di Polacca* in the score, exists also in a separate, shorter form for piano solo, as the *Polonaise en Rondeau.* Besides the latter's shorter length, some technical patterns and melodic details vary in the two versions (Field making amendments from edition to edition as Chopin was apt to do), and to save discussing the solo Polonaise in addition in the later section on *Other Works,* a number of divergencies will be dealt with here.

The Concerto movement is introduced by a rocking pattern of eight bars in the orchestra, beginning:

which is later made the basis of a slower section, in which the piano weaves arabesques round a theme in the orchestra developed from this motif. First editions of the piano solo omitted the introduction (a later included it), and this version omits the midway theme in E flat minor and the section it introduces (a good deal of it working-out) and the slower section this leads into. Several passages of notably expressive colour and pianistic inventiveness are lost thereby, but there is no denying that the Polonaise is the shapelier and more satisfactory as a movement. Not only is the Concerto Polacca rambling in form, but the main theme is held in it to a looser thread, and is considerably tighter in the solo.

Here is the theme:

The staccatos and the bracketed semiquavers occur in the solo version, but not in the Concerto, where no legato and staccato distinction is indicated, and the quaver G alone is given on the sixth half beat in each of the first two bars. Field begins to decorate the theme at its second sentence:

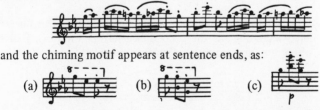

and the chiming motif appears at sentence ends, as:

(a) (b) (c)

the solo version having (a), (b) and (c) at the ends of the first three sentences respectively, and the Concerto movement two (a)s and a (c).

The theme has the sort of jauntiness which those of early Chopin works like the C minor and E flat Rondos, the *Rondo à la Mazur* and the *Krakowiak* display, and one is again conscious of elements, small or larger, which occur also in his music. For instance, if we look at the third bar of Field's theme we find there on the second and third beats the note and rhythmic pattern of the first and second bars of the theme of Chopin's first Rondo:

   Chopin making the addition of a turn.

This is closer still when at the ninth bar Chopin begins his second sentence in E flat major, the notes there being the same as Field's ——— B flat, C, D, E flat and G. There is, too, what feels like an acknowledgement of the basic pattern of Field's previous bar (the dominant, tonic, dominant of the first three notes) in Chopin's introductory bars:

the left hand playing the same in octaves underneath. Small enough elements, it may be said, to be coincidence only, but they are salient motifs in the Field, occurring closely together as in the Chopin, and the whole character of the latter, with its jaunty manner, its skipped patterns and polka bass (to be discussed later), is markedly Field-like.

The nineteenth bar of Field's theme, approached by a semiquaver run up from B flat in the previous bar, is as follows:

which, if again a small element, is closely parallelled by this phrase (in $\frac{4}{4}$ time, beginning on the second beat) from Chopin's E flat Rondo, where the final semiquaver curve is identical:

After giving a version of the theme in G flat major ——— starting it this time with the melody-line of the third bar of the original and so exposing more the pattern which opens the theme of Chopin's first Rondo ——— Field makes a return to the theme in E flat major by the following passage:

In the solo version the treble A flats in each pair of quaver chords are tied and the chords slurred, while the second pair has the F added in the right hand over a repeat of the previous two octaves in the left hand.

Chopin uses this same rhythmic pattern, with its distinctive alternation of running semiquavers and paired chords, in the Grande Polonaise Brillante, to lead back, as Field does, into the first return of the theme, and again later in the movement:

In the E flat Rondo he is to be found using another version of the pattern, the run being longer by four semiquavers so as to fit the pattern into two bars of $\frac{2}{4}$ time:

Further on in the movement Field writes this pattern, rhythmically a fuller version of the earlier:

The first and third bars of this passage differ a little in the solo version, the first bar, for example, being:

In the Grande Polonaise Brillante, Chopin also writes later a fuller version of his first pattern, bearing a striking resemblance to Field's:

Note the same dimished seventh chord in the first bar of each and the same right hand span to the run, G to G, with an E starting note in the left, and also the use by Chopin, as by Field, of contrary motion between the hands, though Chopin takes this the opposite way (outwards from the centre instead of inwards to it). Chopin uses the motif of headlong run followed by two quaver chords again in the Polonaise in E flat minor, Op. 26, No. 2, in this way:

As before, a diminished seventh arpeggio forms the run.

The first section of Field's movement, exploring the main theme, falls into two parts, each rounded off with an orchestral *tutti*. The second *tutti* is the longer in the Polacca; in the solo Polonaise, the first *tutti,* transcribed for the piano, is used both times. In the succeeding section Field makes the contrast of using triplet semi-quaver motion:

In this section not only are Chopin's flying triplets in the Grande Polonaise Brillante called specially to mind, but patterns with direct reflections in that and other of his works occur. In the ninth and tenth bars this motif appears:

Chopin uses the motif thus in the *Alla Polacca* of the *Là ci darem* Variations:

and thus in the first bars of the *Alla Polacca* of the Introduction and Polonaise Brillante for Cello and Piano:

In his solo version Field's ♩♫♫ is phrased like Chopin's, the slurred triplet leading to a staccato on the quaver. The Concerto Polacca, while it contains some if not many dynamics indications (there are a lot more given for the orchestral instruments than for the piano), has very few phrase-marks, indeed only sixteen in the whole movement in the solo part in the *Musica Britannica* score.

In the Field the previous motif is followed by:

with the bass pattern of which we can at once compare this from the
Grande Polonaise Brillante ––– a bar taken at random, Chopin
making considerable use of this bass rhythm in that piece:

He is to be found using this pattern also in works as far apart as the
Cello Polonaise and the Polonaise-Fantasie. At the same time, in the
Field example, the type of chromatic running passage with which
the Grande Polonaise Brillante abounds can be seen in the right
hand.

A repeat of the same phrase a fifth higher in F major, over the
same bass pattern, leads into:

Field's triplet figure of the first bar of this example and his bass are
both found reflected in the Grande Polonaise Brillante. Let us
compare this from the Chopin:

and this also, for another use of the figure followed by a quaver:

The technical pattern shown in the third bar of the Field passage is used by Chopin in the *Alla Polacca* of the *Là ci darem* Variations:

while the Chopin-like character of Field's sliding chromatic progression in the final bar cannot be missed.

Special mention is needed of Field's Polonaise bass patterns and their use by Chopin. Field uses the traditional polonaise rhythm, ♪♪♪♪♪♪ , in the orchestral tuttis (incorporated along with the rhythm into the solo version), but only a few times in the bass of the Polacca's piano part, and most noticeably in this variant:

which occurs, all the same, only four times: twice in tonic harmony and twice in dominant. Indeed, only nine times in the whole Concerto movement does Field fill out the second half of the first beat with semiquavers in the left hand, being far more apt to make these part of the tune-line, as:

The bass pattern last quoted can, however, quickly be noticed in Chopin's Grande Polonaise, where it occurs as:

This in the Field:

parallels this in the Chopin:

and Field's opening bass to the movement (of a rocking figure with a rest on the last quaver of the bar) can be seen reflected in Chopin's opening bass in the Grande Polonaise, with the addition of the semiquaver pulsing of the traditional rhythm on the second half of the first beat. But Chopin noticeably uses the full bass pattern containing the semiquavers less in the earlier Polonaises, and in several either a few times only or not at all.

All these bass patterns of Field's reappear in Chopin: quavers throughout the bar; patterns, with or without semiquavers, stopping short with a final quaver rest; the rhythm of ♪♩ ♫♩; along with Field's various ways of spacing his patterns on the keyboard, e.g. in the disposing of fundamental and higher notes (or chords), the former sometimes on and sometimes off the beat, the use of the rocking pattern and so forth. Here, for comparison with Field's bass pattern in the theme is a final example from Chopin's Polonaise in A flat, Op. 53:

the persistence of this pattern through his Polonaises showing how thoroughly he had absorbed the rocking element present in Field's first bar of the piano part.

Chopin's Prelude No. 15 in D flat is held to embody a particularly original example of his inventiveness, in an idea popularly supposed to have been engendered by the perpetual fall of raindrops outside the window of his room in the monastery at Valldemosa, during his stay with George Sand in Mallorca.

However, not only does the Field movement contain a passage of sixteen bars based on an ostinato octave in the left hand, with a further two bars giving the lower B flat only:

but the middle section (omitted in the solo version) contains the following:

One of the most beautiful of Field's ideas, it would be difficult not to see in the last the basic pattern of this:

and to realize that Chopin's raindrops were Field's beforehand. The falling skipped motif, which is the main element of Chopin's theme, is there too in the Field, as also is the upward stepping by tones (in the rhythm of a minim and a crotchet, to rest on the third note) which follows it --- this element spanning Field's second bar and first beat of the third.

Field's declamatory chord passage leading to the C major section in the Polacca was mentioned earlier, and two bars of the top line shown. Given to the piano alone, here is the complete sequence:

Six bars of quiet chords in the orchestra follow to complete the bridge into the new section, where a theme based on the introductory rocking rhythm is heard in the orchestra, which the piano decorates delicately if simply with passage-work based mainly on arpeggios. This, with its aspect of conforming to shifting chords, shows an approach to Chopin's arpeggio patterning in the first Étude. A particularly charming sequence in this section is the following, in which the manner of Field's arpeggiation is seen in the two final bars:

Having returned to the main theme in its basic key, Field, in the final climax, leading directly into the coda, gives the orchestra this short exclamatory, modulating phrase, taking the music back into E flat major:

In the Grande Polonaise Brillante, in the same place in the movement (i.e. in the final climax) Chopin also gives the orchestra a short exclamatory phrase ――― this twice within the space of five bars, taking the music back into E flat major each time, the second time leading directly into the coda:

Besides conforming in its placing, Chopin's phrase, as can be seen, is strikingly similar to Field's.

Field uses the chiming motif again in the last bars of the solo part:

the orchestra, after the two quaver rests, concluding the movement with an E flat chord, *ff*, in this rhythm: ♫♫ | ♩ ⅞ ⅞ ||.   Chopin uses the same rhythmic pattern to end the Bolero.

In the solo Polonaise Field extends the rhythm to ♫♫ | ♩ ♩ ♩ | ♩ ⅞ ⅞ || in E flat octaves and a final E flat chord, and Chopin uses this rhythm at the end of the Grande Polonaise Brillante.

Diffuseness in structure in the Polacca has been mentioned. Uncertainty of direction in the more extended passages of modulation or transition also shows in that movement, while Field's predilection (in both versions) for the dominant seventh instead of the more direct dominant chord is rather often evident, at such times losing the harmonic foundation needed strength. This was a factor in which his ear noticeably played him false, as Chopin's never did. But the pointers to the future in ideas and technical elements, and especially in Chopin foreshadowings, cannot be overlooked.

When we remember that this piece, as Concerto movement and piano solo, was published in 1816, when Chopin was only six, we can very definitely see it as a jumping-off ground for the later composer's piano Polonaises. Though the solo Polonaise-Rondo makes use only of the material depending on the main theme, with the E flat minor and C major sections omitted, it is still a longer piano work (seven minutes in duration) of approximately the same length as Chopin's longer Polonaises, such as the ones in A flat major and F sharp minor and the Grande Polonaise Brillante, its stylistic affinities with the latter being, as we have seen, hard to miss.

(Concerto No. 4)

In discussing the first three Concertos, and earlier, a good deal has been said about Field's construction of his movements, his visible difficulties in this respect providing a reason for the neglect of the Concertos as concert pieces. So it is not proposed, in the case of the remaining four works in this form, to go into details of structure unless a special point presents itself, but to concentrate on giving elements in the works which appear also in Chopin.

To give the main themes of each movement, even where these

may show no special facet relative to the subject in hand, would all the same seem necessary, not only to satisfy those who do not like a basic theme to be omitted, but also because Field will often transform a simple idea by the embellishment he later adds to it.

The first subject of the first movement of the fourth Concerto, in E flat major like the first and third, shows again the Field, and Chopin, fingerprint of falling and then rising:

The piano enters with a declamatory statement, the most fertile element of which proves to be the arabesque in the fourth bar:

Though this may not at first particularly suggest Chopin, it is interesting to compare the declamatory piano entry in the first movement of his E minor Concerto, which also contains the rhythm ♫♪ | ♩ followed by three strong crotchet chords and a flourish of an uneven number of notes (this upward instead of down-ward) of which the first two notes are the leading-note and the tonic and the remainder arpeggio as in Field's arabesque.

Lyrical relief is provided when, on the last beat of the eighth bar, Field's *cantilena* makes an appearance, a bar and a quarter of this being followed by a descending phrase of filagree decoration, sparkling and chromatic. The second appearance of this in the recapitulation (in the same key) is given here, Field this time varying the first bar with a more chromatic bass and a more curving line in the right hand and starting the second bar on C instead of B flat. The expressive leap of a ninth in the right hand between the first and second bars, which appears also in Field's first Nocturne and

Chopin's Étude Op. 25, No. 1, may be noted:

The bracketed notes in the second bar show the bass notes in the earlier appearance.

Arabesques derived from the one in the last bar of the piano's entry surround this lyrical passage. The following example shows two of these – – – the first resembling patterns previously illustrated from the Polacca of the third Concerto and the *Polonaise en Rondeau* and from Chopin's Polonaise in E flat minor, Op. 26, No. 2, with Field's repeated 'raindrop' bass again showing, while the second arabesque reverts to the piano's original pattern in this movement.

At the twenty-first bar after its entry the piano has the following:

One has only to play this passage to hear Chopin — — — in the melancholy yearning of the first bars, the *cantilena* and the running patterns (both decorative and rounded as with that composer) which remain always melodic. Where Liszt's decorative and *bravura* patterns are usually more straddling, Field's and Chopin's show the same accent on curves instead of angularity and the same elegance. There is also a romantic fervour in the mood which Weber, for instance, a composer in transition between the classical and the romantic, never quite reached, and which is very definitely Field's contribution.

These bars from the Polonaise-Fantasie, compared with bars four and five in particular of the Field, will show the stylistic similarity:

The second subject shows again Field's *cantilena*:

and

Not only does the triplet figuration in the second excerpt give a clear feeling of Chopin (compare his use of similar triplet patterning in the Berceuse), but the subject possesses a gentle melancholy which becomes even more apparent when the theme is put into the minor in the development:

In Field's music, as in Chopin's, characteristic patterns reappear. In these bars from the rounding-off of the exposition after the second subject we see again a specific device (in the first bar) shown in the passage which forms the Introduction to this book and discussed, with reflections in Chopin, in the sections on the Nocturnes:

The development particularly contains a lot of brilliant passage work, working up from a *mf* beginning:

The pattern just given (a variant of that in the first bar of the previous) receives, for instance, this amplification:

this leading, after a few bars, into:

Elements contained in the last two examples are to be found linked by Chopin in the following passage from the F minor Ballade ———— the wide-stepping pattern of the former and an extended falling figure closely similar to that in the latter:

There is, too, in the former Field example, just a hint of the engaging phrase in Chopin's A flat Ballade:

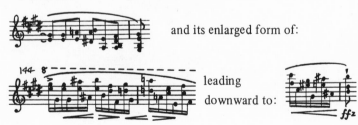

and its enlarged form of:

leading

downward to:

Still from the development, a charming and graceful variant of Field's waving patterns in this section is the following, involving a three against two cross-rhythm:

Two further short excerpts, from Field's climax in this section (and from this movement), may perhaps be permitted:

and

As Harold C. Schonberg said of Chopin's *bravura* passages, Field's (though his textures were generally simpler) were invariably melodic and functional.

The slow movement is a Siciliano, marked *Poco Adagio,* gentle and plaintive, and somewhat Mendelssohn-like in character. Here is the opening, the orchestra having the first three and a half bars:

Field does not, however, leave his line unembellished, and characteristic figures and grace-notes like those in the following excerpts give it variety:

and

The Siciliano is a charming movement, showing the composer once more in a nostalgic mood, and one which, but for its brevity and an ending which is plainly leading to the next movement, might well have found a place among the Nocturnes. Field prepared a solo version of it which was, however, never published.

The Rondo is again in Field's light-hearted mood. While there is a certain suavity in the theme, the decorative elements in the movement contain more pointers towards later piano music. As a basic mood for the themes of his quick movements, this style only showed deepening in the finale of the second Concerto, to a lesser extent in the Polacca of the third, and in the *'à la mazur'* Rondo of the seventh (written much later than the preceding first movement), where it gained a greater seriousness. In Chopin's music, the style, evident in a number of earlier works, soon gave way to one with more weight (here we must not forget that he was born twenty-eight years after Field).

The movement is opened by the piano, with this theme:

to which Field is soon adding characteristic embellishments, such as:

and convoluted triplet running passages such as those illustrated from the Polacca of the third Concerto. The affinity between the figuration in the last passage and in this from Chopin's Rondo in E flat will be obvious:

At a later appearance Field gives his theme a drop of a semitone such as Chopin gives to his in the Rondo of his E minor Concerto:

In his movement Chopin runs up towards the return of his theme as if to give it in its original key of E major (the preceding chord, in the left hand, being a dominant seventh on B), but gives it in E flat instead, working it back into E major in the following way:

In the middle section of the Polonaise in A flat, Op. 53, Chopin uses the device again and drops his theme suddenly by a semitone from E major into E flat major, returning to E major and making the same change a second time.

Bravura patterns and rounded-off episodes of the same types as have been exampled from the Rondos of the two previous Field Concertos occur again in this movement, with again Chopin implications if in this case fewer particular reflections. Among the motifs and patterns which do have reflections some resemble ones in the Polacca of the third Concerto adjusted to fit into $\frac{2}{4}$ instead of $\frac{3}{4}$, and so there is no need to example or discuss them in addition, unless they present a new or specially interesting complexion. One meriting mention would seem to be the triplet octave pattern seen in the Polacca, used in this movement in the left hand in a modulating section of forty-four bars:

Among technical patterns having clear affinities with others in Chopin, we can compare this:

with this in the Tarantelle:

and again, in the Field, this:

and this:

with this in the Cello and Piano Polonaise:

These triplet patterns in the Field:

bring again a reminder of similar flying triplet figures in the Grande Polonaise Brillante, while Field's chiming motif appears again at the end of the movement:

rounded-off by three strong E flat chords. In both Field and Chopin this motif seems to carry the particular implication of E flat major.

(Concerto No. 5)

The fifth Concerto, in C major, bears the title of *L'Incendie par l'Orage*.

The first movement opens with a tremolo, *ff*, on C, spread over five octaves from the C immediately below the bass clef to that just above the treble, and of this duration:

The first subject, beginning at the fourth bar, is played quietly by the strings, horn and bassoon:

There are thirty-one bars of quiet material like this, leading to the following Polonaise-like theme, which constitutes a bridge passage between first and second subjects:

The second subject has a line and rhythmic pattern almost exactly the same as the first subject, with the difference that it begins on the third of the scale instead of the tonic. In the orchestral introduction it is in the same key as the first subject: C major. In the solo part in the exposition it is in the more usual dominant key, which will be illustrated.

The solo part of this movement bears the look of Chopin on the page more strikingly than any of Field's concerto movements so far. The piano's entry is a terse declamatory statement:

which bears a relationship in type with Chopin's solo entry in the first movement of the E minor Concerto, if for a closer reflection this, from the posthumously published Polonaise in G sharp minor, can be exampled:

against which we can also set this from Field's development (his version there of the piano's entry – – – though this appears quite late in the section, after the working up to and presentation of the first part of the storm, a 'whirlwind' which takes the music into C minor):

The C major example (the entry) exhibits the drop from a higher key-note on the first beat on to a lower on the second beat which also appears in the Chopin excerpt, while the last example shows a convoluted decorative pattern similar to the succeeding figure in the Chopin, with the difference that Field's figure goes upwards whereas Chopin's comes downwards.

The movement contains a number of specifically Chopin-like patterns and textures. One pattern

has been exampled in the discussion of the first movement of the second Concerto, along with a variant in grouping (four semiquavers instead of semiquaver triplets) from that movement. Chopin, as was then noted, is to be found using the pattern in the first Concerto and the fourth Ballade.

In the following the floating melody above the widespread bass and the langorous mood unmistakably foreshadow the same effect in Chopin, used by him how many times in how many works, especially the Nocturnes:

The grace-notes at the beginning of the second bar are specially revealing.

The next example shows Field writing particularly attractive display passages for the piano:

Chopin, in the Fantasie, duplicates the pattern shown in the third bar, with the difference that he begins the triplet a note earlier, so changing the accentation:

Elsewhere Chopin begins the pattern with a falling instead of a rising semitone, as:

but in C major, and in G major, he follows Field's shape.

The second subject, which, as has been explained, is really a close variant of the movement's first theme, is given this treatment in the piano part:

Still from the exposition, the following phrase is one which has clear links with others in Chopin:

The following, from the Cello Polonaise, will illustrate this:

Similarly, the next examples have affinity with convoluted and chromatic patterns seen in Chopin:

(a)

which leads, at the seventh bar, to:

(b)

The exposition closes with a trill in chords, the left hand playing those with the tails turned upward:

Here we have an enlargement by Field of the traditional device of closing the main sections of concerto movements with a trill.

The development section has a declamatory opening, which gives way after a few bars to a more lyrical mood. At the tenth bar this pattern appears:

A motif again of which Chopin made considerable use, the following from the C sharp minor Scherzo provides a particularly effective example:

while another example is to be found in the slow movement of the E minor Concerto:

At the fifty-fourth bar of the development, with a change into C minor, *l'Orage* begins. Most of these intervening bars, following the last example (in B flat) quoted, are taken up with a pattern of running semiquavers, marked *f* and suggesting a strongly blowing wind:

By the thirteenth bar of the C minor section the storm is in full blast, conveyed mainly by a pattern similar to the triplet figure in the Polacca of the third Concerto and chromatic runs:

Like the first movements of the second and third Concertos, this movement is one which has a good many key-changes, and at the end of the development the following figure occurs. The mood is now quiet again and the orchestral accompaniment *p*, with the tension relaxed and the storm clearly dying down:

Here again there is a link with a figure in Chopin, who writes the following in the development of the first movement of the E minor Concerto:

Towards the end of the movement the following bars deserve to be quoted for their combination of the scintillating and the delicate:

The concluding passages contain again Field's chiming motif:

this being followed by scale and arpeggio runs, a trill in chords between the hands, the pattern:

which Chopin, too, uses chromatically in the nineteenth bar of the *Là ci darem* Variations, and a run in chords:

The movement is then rounded off by a final eight bars for the orchestra.

The slow movement is a gentle and very short *Adagio* (38 bars), its technical basis the same as that of the slow movement of Beethoven's 'Pathetique' Sonata:

It has a clear sonority and in the first bar shows the aspect of falling (a semitone) before it begins to rise, but, while it gives an interesting sidelight on Field's links with the classical tradition, it does not exhibit his personal romantic colouring and pianistic inventiveness in the same way as do the slow movements of the second and sixth Concertos (and even that of the first) and the G major interlude in the first movement of the seventh.

All the same, there is a Chopin implication in its first bar and a half, that of the opening of the Étude in E major, Op. 10, No. 3:

Apart from the addition of an up-beat, Chopin's motif follows the same outline as Field's on the same degrees of the scale, with the same accompaniment pattern played by the right hand under the melody. The differences are the left hand's syncopated pattern fitting with the right hand's semiquavers and the double pace at which Chopin takes the melodic unit against the accompanying figure: ♫♩ instead of ♩ ♫ | ♩ ; the basis of both motifs is nevertheless the same, with a similar accordance in tempo markings.

The main theme of the Rondo is again in Field's lighter vein:

The movement does not lack elements such as have already been seen and discussed, but none makes a particular new point until we come to an interlude in $\frac{6}{8}$ time. The section opens with a rocking rhythm on a repeated chord:

which gives a strong suggestion of the start of Chopin's F major Ballade:

the rocking basis continuing throughout this interlude as through the opening section of the Ballade. Field, we may remember, used this rocking rhythm on a single note to bring back the theme in the *Grande Pastorale* (Nocturne No. 17). In the present section, after two bars of the repeated chord a floating theme is introduced above the rocking basis, exactly as in the Ballade, during the course of which this expressive phrase appears:

Have we not heard something like it in Chopin? Certainly we have. It is not too much to say that all Field's most interesting ideas proved fertile in Chopin's hands, and here is its unmistakable reflection in the Scherzo of the B flat minor Sonata:

In the Field the orchestra supports and reinforces the solo part with the rocking rhythm on the strings and the tune-line on the clarinet.

The opening portion of the interlude is succeeded by fifty-four and a half bars of delicate semiquaver figuration in the solo part for the right hand, the first bar and a half consisting of a turn linked to a chromatic upward run, leading to:

The rocking rhythm is here resumed, and kept up by the left hand in the middle of the keyboard till the C pedal note (which, reintroduced, is retained to the end) is dropped an octave and the bass pattern filled in to become:

That there is a measure of chromaticism in the chord movement, and not merely a tonic and dominant basis for the left hand and the right hand's decorative line, may be judged from the last example.

In this portion of the interlude the orchestra supports the solo part by reproducing the accompanying pattern ––– the strings as well as the piano's left hand have the rocking rhythm. Field does not, however, give the orchestra any part of the previous melody-line to play against the piano's decorative passage-work, though one might have expected this, but just allows the clarinet and bassoon to contribute wisps of melody from time to time:

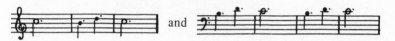

The piano's semiquaver patterning in the right hand varies from the chromatic and closely curving to the more widely spread, such as:

and if the interlude as a whole is less confidently shaped than that in the first movement of the seventh Concerto, it displays a very personal delicacy and gracefulness.

A particularly charming and inventive piece of filagree, across the basic $\frac{6}{8}$ rhythm, ends the section:

The concluding twelve bars of the piano part in the Rondo exhibit a striking and novel keyboard pattern:

downward with a cadence on to a C major chord and rising again to:

Again we have a device used later by Chopin, in this from the Cello Polonaise:

and this from the F major Ballade:

The interesting and effective way in which Field moves away from the basic key with the very last chord of his piano part forms a true 'surprise' cadence, and one not the same as the usual 'interrupted.' Beginning with this E dominant seventh chord in the first inversion, the orchestra has fifteen bars of *ff* material with which it rounds off the movement.

(Concerto No. 6)

The sixth Concerto, like the fifth, is in C major.

The theme, by its marching nature, fits into a specific Field, and Chopin, category:

Here one can think of the theme of the first movement of Chopin's
Cello Sonata which, though it is in the minor, follows a similar
rhythmic- and note-pattern: starting from the fifth note of the scale
on an up-beat leading to the third of the scale on the first beat of the
first bar, it then falls, like Field's theme, through a sixth to the
dominant, before the line rises again at the third bar:

Peter Gould, writing in Dr. Alan Walker's book on Chopin (1966) is
of the opinion that "One can almost hear the orchestra in the
opening four bars."

Field's seventh bar contains his familiar skipped pattern:

A little later in the orchestral introduction he makes use of a
device consisting of a melodic element repeated over and over above
changing chords:

this element being repeated through nine bars (i.e. eighteen times)
before it falls by steps through two bars to middle C.

Chopin, too, had a liking for the device, the Mazurka in D major,
Op. 33, No. 2, providing this example:

Chopin repeats his two-bar element eight times, moving back into his basic key of D major by means of a G natural in place of the A in the right hand and respaced left hand chords in the sixteenth bar.

The entry of the solo instrument in Field's movement shows a device familiar in romantic piano concerto writing: right and left hands play a melodic line (which derives from the first subject instead of being a restatement or embellished version of it) an octave apart in the upper part of the keyboard while the orchestra accompanies:

This is followed after two bars by:

The Rondo of Chopin's E minor Concerto contains an example:

The opening section of the *Krakowiak* (the hands here two octaves apart) and its second subject, the finale of his F minor Concerto and also the first movements of the Scriabin Concerto and Rachmaninoff's No. 3 supply other examples.

Sixteen bars after its entry Field begins giving the piano characteristic decorative passages.

The following, occurring shortly before the second subject, shows him writing a rather more straddling pattern with, this time, Lisztian implications:

It seems probable that the two F semiquavers for the right hand on the first half of beat two in the second bar are misprints for E (the latter giving an octave fall matching that in the previous patterns), and the lower F in the last chord in the left hand may similarly be a misprint for D.

Coming just after the second subject, the next example contains a ' dog-running-after-its tail ' figure which also finds a place in Chopin's music. A pattern which we have seen Field using before (in the second Concerto), he fits it here into the following phrase:

Whereas earlier the melody-line only of Chopin's D flat major ' Minute ' Waltz was given, here is the full texture, from which may be seen the close conformity of his overall patterning in this with Field's:

The second subject shows again Field's *cantilena* manner:

as does this, early in the development:

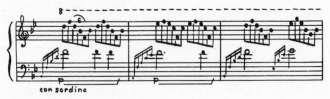

Again there is a feeling of Liszt.

While it might be thought that some measure of Field-Chopin

correspondences could be coincidence, it could hardly be true of so many, and it could certainly not be of the next to be given. A *bravura* figure which first appears near the end of Field's exposition gives rise to the following in the development:

a variant of the first bar being:

Who, one wonders, can miss the link between this striking idea and the basic pattern and mood of Chopin's Étude in A minor, Op. 25, No. 11:

This is indeed one of the most startling instances of Field anticipating Chopin, or, looked at in reverse, of Chopin being indebted to Field for the fundamental idea on which he built a piece: this Étude. The key is the same: A minor, and Field's individual rhythmic bass pattern is reproduced. In the right hand his motif is speeded up into groups of six instead of four semiquavers, as we have seen Chopin do with other Field figures. Knowing what we do of Chopin's knowledge of, use of, and admiration for Field's music (discussed earlier), can it really be doubted that these passages in the Concerto gave rise to Chopin's eleventh Etude in his second set?

Edgar Stillman Kelly compares Chopin's opening motif with Beethoven's ♪♫♫|♩ of the fifth Symphony for dramatic effect, but has seen no Field connection, obviously not knowing this Concerto by that composer.

Field leads from the recapitulation into the coda of this movement by means of a delicate falling figure based on the turn:

to which a comparable figure in Chopin's music is this in the C major Rondo:

The bracketed semiquavers a third below the upper line appear in the left hand of the first piano part in the two-piano version, giving the sense of a dual line in thirds which is a feature of the Field passage.

The slow movement, transposed from E into F major, was also published among the Nocturnes as No. 6, and has been discussed in the section devoted to those pieces.

The Rondo is similar in mood and material to that of the fifth Concerto. The theme has the same lighthearted, one might say chirpy, quality:

Field's decorative figures, again, show his very personal inventiveness. Characteristic patterns in the movement, which at the same time call to mind others in Chopin, are the following:

and

Field uses rounded-off sections based on figures such as the former exactly as Chopin does, as episodes between themes, and here is Chopin using an equivalent figure as an episode in the Rondo in C major:

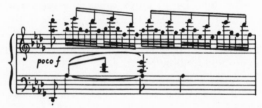

(solo version)

while with the second example we can compare this from the Berceuse:

Field leads into the second appearance of his Rondo theme by the following passage:

After the first beat of the first bar there is no bass to this passage, in which, starting from the top (*), we find the same descending pattern that Chopin uses in the coda of the Finale of the B minor Sonata:

Typical again, a further decorative passage from the Field movement is this:

leading to:

Against the first we can set this from the G flat Polonaise of Chopin:

while he is to be found using the figuration of the second in the
concluding passage of the Tarantelle (this passage along with a
similar figure appearing in the first movement of Field's fourth
Concerto is illustrated in the section dealing with that concerto).

An orchestral link, such as we have seen Field using in the Polacca
of the third Concerto and Chopin in the Grande Polonaise Brillante,
introduces the coda:

The sparkling passage-work for the piano which opens this section
gives way to this tender little phrase:

with the outlay of which we may compare Chopin's treatment of his
second subject in the *Krakowiak*:

After this brief contrast in mood, Field concludes his coda with
further passage-work for the piano, which includes this pattern in
wide arpeggios:

and the following *bravura* figure:

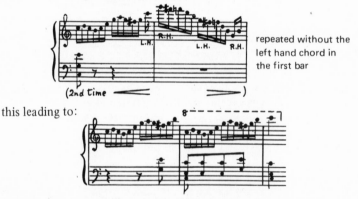

repeated without the
left hand chord in
the first bar

this leading to:

Field's chiming motif may be noticed again in the left hand.
Beginning with the final note of the piano part there are five bars of
rounding-off material for the orchestra.

(Concerto No. 7)

The seventh Concerto is the one of which the French critic, Fétis,
wrote in 1833 that it was "diffuse, but fully of happy ideas." This
Concerto contains undeniably Field's richest, as well as some of his
most sombre, material. As Fétis saw, the shaping is the less
satisfactory part of the work, though, as with the second Concerto,

there is evident, at least in the first movement, a sizeable basic plan. If habitually not very good at links between sections and at achieving watertight modulations when on a larger scale, Field did better than usual in the opening movement, and with a more confident Rondo it could have been his most notable concerto. While the slow G major interlude in the middle of the first movement still shines like a particular jewel (an exquisite nocturne which, published later as a separate item, it indeed became: Nocturne No. 12), the movement, if with a few uneasy corners and displaying episodes rather than much development, contains unquestionably Field's most firmly directed and strongly contrasted material.

The work opens with two drum rolls spaced over four bars:

followed by this striking, romantic and melancholy theme, in which Field's fingerprint of falling and then rising can again be seen:

leading after five bars to:

The second subject also exhibits the falling and rising fingerprint. Here is its basic, simpler outline in the orchestral introduction:

*there is an A flat chord in the lower part here in some copies of the score and similarly when the subject recurs in the solo part.

In the seventh bar the skipped pattern which is a feature in both Field's and Chopin's music can be seen, and Field characteristically embellishes the theme in subsequent appearances. For instance, in the repeat of the opening phrase in the orchestral statement the third bar becomes:

while the piano's first statement of the theme has this at its start:

and this for its fourth and fifth bars:

Over the initial drum pattern played this time on viola and timpanum an octave apart the piano makes its entry with a series of *bravura* flourishes based on arpeggios:

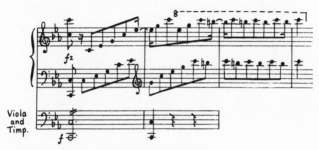

followed by this beautiful, rhapsodic sentence for its very free statement of the first subject:

How laden this is with the melancholy that we have come to regard as exclusively Chopin's, and how its pianistic outlay, phraseology and figuration conform to his. The musician who did not know its source might be pardoned for asking from which of his works it came. From this example alone could there be any doubt that Field was there in this territory beforehand? Though the second and final movement was not added till later and the work as a whole not performed till 1833 in Paris, this movement was already written by 1821. Chopin, still a boy, had at this time written just his first few simple, juvenile pieces.

For the solo instrument Field writes this version of the orchestral introduction's bridge passage material:

The type of treatment accorded the second subject in the piano part we have already seen.

As Chopin's technical and decorative patterns were to do, Field's in this work become more complicated and more varied. There are in this movement brusque rhythmic patterns such as:

patterns in thirds:

and in double thirds:

There are convoluted passages in sixths (as in the last bar of the preceding example) and in tenths:

In setting out the previous examples their order in the movement has been sacrificed, though they are all in the exposition after the second subject. For instance, the last comes before the one shown immediately before it and runs into it after a fourth bar.

A salient element in the last example appears also in Chopin, in this phrase from the Grande Polonaise Brillante:

and like the Field movement the Polonaise contains a great many skipped patterns, one of these being:

Field writes filagree patterns in demi-semiquavers, such as:

and others with a gymnastic aspect, like the following which leaps an octave and returns, leaps and returns:

The G major interlude (Nocturne No. 12), which takes the place of a slow movement in the Concerto (its thematic line deriving from the C minor opening subject), comes between the exposition in this, a delicate and perfect miniature. Excerpts from it are to be found in the section on the Nocturnes, where it has already been discussed. It may, however, be appropriate to repeat here that it was after hearing Field play this Concerto in 1833 that Chopin added the Andante *Spianato* to his Grande Polonaise Brillante.

After this tender and dreamlike interlude, with its truly *spianato* accompaniment figure, the movement awakens again with the development, which begins with an arpeggio-based flourish in G minor for the solo instrument after the pattern of its first entry, but still contains, after forty-six bars of *bravura* material, another near—dreamy, if up to pace, interlude in A major.

Contrapuntal elements gain ground, too, in the movement. Here, showing this aspect, is a *bravura* passage from the development, with Chopin implications not only in the chromatic semiquaver groups but also in the chords and their ostinato accompaniment:

The following passage shows Field writing a dual vocal line in counterpoint round a double trill:

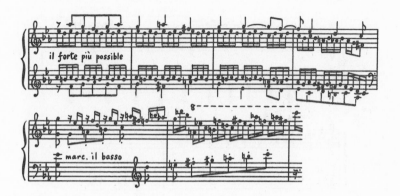

His running basses appear again, being as much a feature of his music as of Chopin's, while the greater luxuriance in his figuration is shown again in this *bravura* passage from the coda, in which the contrapuntal aspect is once more evident:

An affinity with the pattern contained in the first bar is shown by this, from Chopin's Nocturne in F minor, Op. 55, No. 1:

The piano part concludes with this florid passage and final trill:

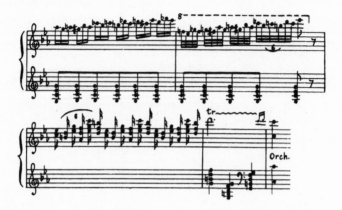

The final C octaves, which begin the short concluding *tutti*, are played by the orchestra alone, the piano part ending with the last D in the previous bar.

Like Field, Chopin in both his Concertos seeks ways of amplifying the conventional concluding trill for the solo instrument of the classical composers.

The second and final movement, besides being a Rondo and titled thus, is in Mazurka style, a new departure for Field. Here there could be a reverse influence from Chopin to Field, for, though neither of the former's Concertos appeared till after 1833 (when the whole Field Concerto was heard), a number of his Mazurkas had already been published. All the same, Field's way of handling his themes and his technical patterns accord with established features of his style. The word *mazurka* may say Chopin to us, but the manner is still Field's.

The movement's disadvantage is its diffuse shape, with passages which over-hug keys, pauses, and key-shifts that seem arbitrarily made and not dictated by any special plan in the course and purpose of the music ——— so that otherwise interesting ideas and technical patterns are robbed of much of their impact.

Having said the above, it needs to be added that the ideas which Fétis called "happy," and which are an extension of Field's range, do indeed abound. It is unfortunate that they should be fitted into an unsatisfactory structure, the recurring aspect which has led to so much of Field's music being forgotten and the importance of his innovations overlooked.

After an orchestral opening of sixteen bars, beginning:

the piano presents the main theme:

After four statements of the theme divided by short episodes, we have a *tutti* beginning:

which, were we not told was by Field, we might easily assume came from a Chopin Mazurka. Here, for comparison with the curve which rounds off Field's phrase, are two of Chopin's sentence endings from his Mazurkas, the first from the one in B flat, Op. 17, No. 1:

and the second from the posthumous Mazurka in C major in the
.Breitkopf and Härtel edition (its two final bars):

Even should it be a case this time of Field nodding in Chopin's
direction and following his lead, there is still no mistaking the
stylistic affinity. Note again the fall and then rise in Field's melodic
shape, both between one bar and the next and in the overall line.

    Melodic and decorative ideas which one feels should be exampled
in the order in which they occur in the Rondo are the following:

(a)

(b)

(c)

Note the dog-running-after-its-tail pattern in bars 5 and 6 of the last example.

(d)

(e)

(f)

In the last can be seen a pattern of a type Chopin used in the 'Black Keys' Étude in G flat, Op. 10, No. 5, with the difference that

Chopin spreads his pattern over three octaves for two bars, then reducing it to two octaves for a further two bars, and that his basic triplet describes an upward instead of a downward arc:

(g) The next idea occurs in two sections which possess more feeling of development than other sections in the movement:

and

then the same a fourth lower in B flat minor leading to:

Here we can set against Field's last pattern (g) this from Chopin's
Rondo à la Mazur:

As a preparation for his coda, Field interrupts the ¾ time and
mazurka rhythm with a short *Adagio* in 4/4.
This is based on a skipped pattern:

and does not approach the interest or expressiveness of the G major
interlude in the first movement. Clearly he wanted to throw into
relief his final section and its *bravura* passage-work for the solo
instrument, but there seems no real reason for an *adagio,* particularly
such an inexpressive one. A pause would have done as well. Chopin
manages this better with the repeated horn call (which perforce has
to be taken at a slightly slower tempo) with which he introduces the
closing section in the finale of his F minor Concerto.

In his coda Field employs a variant of the motif consisting of a
run followed by two chords, usually declamatory, which we have
seen both him and Chopin use (examples are given earlier from the
Polacca of Field's third Concerto and Chopin's Grande Polonaise
Brillante and E flat Rondo):

Bars fifteen and sixteen of the coda show Field writing the
following technical pattern:

Chopin uses the same device in the coda of the finale of the F minor Concerto:

Field's coda consists of thirty-two bars, the piano's exhuberant final pattern being:

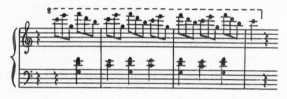

A terse orchestral *tutti* of four bars then concludes the section and the movement.

In this second movement Field seems especially unable adequately to prepare for his ideas as they succeed each other, or to develop them logically once he has introduced them. So much in the movement equates with Chopin, from the mazurka theme to innumerable decorative patterns with the same aspects of elegance and brilliance, yet Chopin's consistently superior handling of his material is left evident by Field's uncertainty in this direction.

Fétis's judgment of the seventh Concerto, as "diffuse, but full of happy ideas," is basically true of all the Concertos. Field, who could devise truly exquisite smaller modulations, was more often than not at sea when it came to managing these on a larger scale, and again and again when the music seems to be moving somewhere the ear is upset by trite cadences and back-slidings to the basic key, by melodic lines suddenly cut short, and unmistakable signs of his not knowing where to go next. It is his misfortune that a series of happy ideas (and highly original ones) cannot alone make a convincing larger work ――― there has to be some sense of developing and weaving these into a plan. Here Chopin's superiority can at once be seen. Though an inordinate number of his technical devices and turns of phrase, rhythms and sonorities, and indeed the very way he used the keyboard, came from Field, he had a strong, if idiosyncratic, sense of structure. And though Field's sense of the orchestra was far greater than Chopin's and his Concertos have full and imaginative orchestral parts, the Chopin two, despite their dull orchestral accompaniments, emerge as more satisfactory through the completeness of their piano parts, and so remain in performance. In Chopin's the piano, once it has entered, says everything, and with complete confidence, whereas in those of Field both piano and orchestra share in an over-frequent lack of direction in the music. One feels that the Field Concertos need someone to straighten them out ––– someone who could achieve the structural balance necessary without sacrificing any of the freshness and originality of the ideas. Plain cutting would accomplish some of this, if by no means all. Opposing editions show considerable variation in passages and contains suggestions for cuts of various lengths, revealing that the composer himself did not feel too certain of the works' definitive shaping.

Field made solo versions of a number of movements from the Concertos, probably not merely for the purpose of having them in a solo form, but also to try to achieve in them a more balanced structure. In shortening the longer movements he usually made them more shapely, while sometimes sacrificing particularly telling ideas, such as the theme of the $\frac{6}{8}$ section in the Rondo of the fifth Concerto, which contained piquant melodic elements, and the 'rain-drops' passage in the Polacca of the third Concerto when constructing the *Polonaise en Rondeau*. The latter was the only one of these versions to be published. Depending on their degree of balance and effectiveness we might perhaps see others in print in the future.*

*These versions are not the same as the separate movements of Concertos published without accompaniment parts (i.e. as piano solos) at usually the same time or not long after the full works. A compressed version of the Rondo of the 6th Concerto 'arranged and edited' by A. Marschan and published in 1853 (London) would seem unlikely to be Field's own.

8.
Hummel (1778–1837).

Though the purpose of this book is to discuss Field and Chopin, a section on Hummel may not be out of place. In support of the need at least to examine Hummel's music we have Nieck's statement that almost all of the peculiarities of Chopin's early virtuosic style are to be found in the works of Field and Hummel, and we know, too, that one of the concertos the Polish composer most admired was Hummel's in A minor, Op. 85.

The earlier part of Hummel's output resembled Mozart more than any other composer, and then a change came over his style midway in his career, when a more romantic vein began to appear. Evident first in the Polacca of *La Bella Capricciosa,* Op. 55 (Introduction and *Alla Polacca*), and more noticeable in the Rondo Brillant for Piano and Orchestra, Op. 56* (both published in 1815), this reached its full expression in the A minor Concerto.

To look first at the Rondo Brillant: after a slow introduction containing a good deal of sensitive and elegant embellishment of the melodic line, Hummel presents a main theme which approximates in its light-hearted nature to themes of Field's in similar movements:

There are a number of pointers to Chopin in the work: for example, in sections of arpeggio passage-work fitting modulating chords such as Chopin writes in the *Krakowiak* and in the Rondo in C, Op. 73, and in a technical pattern such as the following:

Grove's Dictionary lists this as for Piano Solo and omits it from the works for piano and orchestra. A solo copy was also published (the two versions being 56a and 56b respectively) but this still contains the instrumental indications.

against which can be set this, from Chopin's posthumously published Polonaise in F minor, Op. 71, No. 3:

There are many instances of such 'patterns on two levels' in Chopin's works. The opening of the third Écossaise shows another, as also does the end, the latter pattern being written:

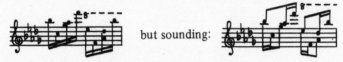

but sounding:

and there are stretches of some bars in the first movement of the F minor Concerto, to name but one more example.

The following *bravura* passage from Hummel's Rondo:

set against this in Chopin's Allegro de Concert:

would appear at the very least to be a skeleton outline for the latter, while Chopin's following phrase:

could similarly owe something to bars 3 and 4 of Hummel's theme (the first quotation). Again, this, at the end of Hummel's first full statement of his theme (bars 23—36 after the piano's entry):

would seem as definite a model as one could find for this of Chopin's at the end of his first thematic paragraph for the piano in the Rondo of his first Concerto (bars 27—31):

If Hummel's Rondo Brillant exhibits pointers to elements in Chopin's music, in the A minor Concerto (published in 1821) we have much which possesses the full flavour. The haunting strain of poetic melancholy in this Concerto appears in scarcely any other work, though there is a lesser approach to it in the B minor Concerto (No. 2), which is harder and brighter and considerably less persuasive. Clearly among Hummel's works the former Concerto made the most impact on Chopin and, if Field's A flat Concerto served him as a model for his No. 2 in F minor (particularly the latter's first movement), it would seem beyond reasonable doubt that Hummel's No. 1 in A minor had more than a little to say in the forming of the main movement of his first Concerto in E minor.

To set the orchestral openings of the two works together, here is Hummel's:

Chopin's being:

the first phrase of
eight bars ending in:

Note the correspondence in character and the common elements bracketed in the two examples. The flavour of Chopin is indeed so strong in Hummel's theme that it could easily have come from the Polish composer's pen. The similarities would appear to be too close to be mere coincidence: not only do pertinent melodic turns of phrase in Hummel's subject appear in Chopin's, but the first three bass notes are the same in each ——— tonic, mediant, tonic.

Hummel's first eight bars are followed by a plaintive little phrase:

which is repeated with varied (chromatic) chords, and given this
treatment later in the piano:

One wonders at once where one may have heard it, or something like
it, before, and then recollects a phrase of Chopin's in the same
position in the Allegro de Concert ——— following the two opening
phrases of the theme:

This is, like Hummel's phrase, repeated, with a little difference in the
bass line the second time.

If we find a similarity between Hummel's and Chopin's first
subjects, what are we to think of the next two examples? Hummel's
bridge-passage material for the solo instrument contains an episode
beginning thus:

while Chopin begins his bridge material in this manner:

Where this passage recurs in the recapitulation (in the same key) he ends its second 4-bar phrase with a repeated note after the fashion of Hummel's phrase-endings (marked with asterisks in both examples):

Again coincidence? On this evidence alone it would appear undeniable that Hummel's ideas and methods in this Concerto had made an impression on the later composer.

Another element, a technical pattern with which Hummel makes further play in the development, occurs first in the *bravura* passage leading into the just-quoted episode:

while Chopin is to be found writing this in the Rondo for two pianos:

Before leaving this movement a further passage asks to be quoted. To appreciate its flavour and understand how forcibly Hummel presented what we have been in the habit of regarding as essentially a Chopin mood ——— of an exquisite nostalgia, and in the same terms ——— the whole passage (which leads into the coda, starting at the Tempo I) needs to be given:

In the ninth, tenth and eleventh bars of the coda Hummel gives his units of a semiquaver triplet and a quaver an upward direction:

in these bars particularly anticipating Chopin's use of an equivalent figure in the Bolero, where the key is also A minor:

Again, the technical device shown at the opening of Hummel's coda ——— a chromatic moving line against a repeated note in the same hand ——— was one which Chopin made use of later in the coda of the F major Ballade, the key of the section concerned being once more A minor:

Indeed, this progression of Chopin's would seem to be a combination of the last two patterns of Hummel's: the technical device of the first plus the falling modulatory scheme of the second.

The slow movement, a stately Larghetto in $\frac{3}{4}$ time, has a cooler manner, rather like Beethoven in a serene mood, if it exhibits a luxuriantly embellished line. There is no strain here until, in a few of the last phrases and in the cadenza linking this movement to the third, a little of the nostalgia creeps back again. This is one of the phrases:

Does one again detect a suggestion of Field (an aspect to be touched on later) in the falling figure of which that composer, and later Chopin, made considerable use?

With the Rondo the full melancholy returns, in a theme of which
Chopin might have been proud ———— it stays in the mind along with
his most expressive:

The bass of the opening, and also the following from the theme's
second appearance, display the type of complex setting out (of even
quite simple textures) which is such a feature of Chopin's notation:

While I have not seen this particular aspect detailed previously (that
is, Chopin's notational complexity related to Hummel's), Herbert
Weinstock, the American writer, states that "very often Chopin's
figurations and simpler harmonic motions are those of a composer
who could scarcely have composed exactly that way if he had
remained unacquainted with Hummel's music."

It is certainly an original touch of Hummel's to give a Rondo
theme this aspect of a plaintive gravity in place of the customary
jollity. One wonders how much this subject (and the movement also)
may have had to do with setting the style of Chopin's C major
Rondo, particularly the second subject of the latter, which uses the
same notes as Hummel's ———— G sharp, A and E ———— in its two

opening phrases:

Even the span and the notes of Chopin's first subject appear later in a phrase for the piano:

while an individual technical pattern which brings two notes together at the end of an arpeggio of six semiquavers played in triplets:

is repeated in this manner in the original solo version of the Chopin piece:

In its later appearances, Hummel gives his main subject delicate and entirely credible Chopin-like ornaments and embellishment, while his second, both as to its type and manner of writing out, has obvious Chopin connotations:

as, too, does the following:

Both the first and third movements of the Concerto feature codas built from separate ideas such as Chopin wrote (for example, in the first, second and fourth Ballades). Hummel, though, does bring into the coda of his Rondo (in the orchestra) an allusion to the first subject before he ends the section and the movement.

This final coda, at *Doppio movimento,* has a particularly *bravura* aspect, and exhibits, among a number of individual technical patterns, two, each of which has a special reference to one of Chopin's Études. The first is:

Chopin uses the same idea in this manner in the Étude in A minor, Op. 10, No. 2:

The second pattern is:

There would seem little doubt that this figure of Hummel's formed the basis of the following in Chopin's Étude in C sharp minor, Op. 10, No. 4 (bar 2 of the theme and its later repeats):

and also:

Chopin may again be seen to be finding inspiration for pieces in figures which have particularly appealed to him in Hummel's, as in Field's, music. The basis once selected (if selected can be the right word for what must have been to a large extent an involuntary process), that the end-product was always so convincingly shaped is a tribute to his integrity and the reason why his music holds the position it does today.

Both Hummel's codas have a study-like complexion, are brilliant in style besides being shaped with conviction, and one can at once hear a link between them and Chopin's manner in the more brilliant of his Études.

Hummel's *bravura* technical writing clearly had an influence on Chopin, if his sole equalling of the Chopin (and the Field) quality in the music (that is, in dignity and full expressiveness) was in this Concerto, especially the first and third movements, where the complexion of his musical thought was also to have its influence. Too, Hummel in this one work (that is, among that Romantic part of his output) was to score, in a way Field did not, by his far more cohesive handling of his material. Though the slow movement has less colour and a cooler character, it has serenity and a lot of filagree decoration suiting the instrument. But the Concerto has seriousness and assurance, and is sensitive to a degree not equalled by any other work of his. A singularly well-balanced work, Chopin's admiration of which can well be understood, it is incomprehensible that it has not a stable place in the concert hall today. Here one suspects that the isolated nature of the composer's achievement in this work accounts for its neglect. A recording, issued by Vox, is available now (and also of the B minor Concerto), though in a badly cut version, which manages to lose quite a lot of the best passages and reduce the impact of the climaxes, if it still allows one to appreciate the basic quality of the music. This is a pity, but Hummel is not, of course, regarded with the same reverence as Beethoven or Tschaikovsky. More difficult to obtain, there is (or was) a foreign recording, uncut, with Artur Balsam as soloist.

Chopin, though, did not learn anything in the way of balance between piano and orchestra from Hummel's Concerto, any more than he had from those of Field. His own orchestral accompaniments remained inadequate and unimaginative, hindering rather than helping the solo part, in sharp contrast to the excellence of Hummel's orchestral part. The middle section of the latter's last movement, for instance, is made up of a flowing melody which the piano first accompanies with a waving figure in triplet semiquavers, then shares in, then decorates in the upper part of the keyboard with sparkling figuration and scale passages, again in semiquaver triplets.

Here it is interesting to note that Gerald Abraham considers Chopin's perfunctory treatment of the orchestra in his Concertos must be attributed not only to his unhappiness in handling it, but to the example of his model, Hummel, whom he considers passed on this type of restricted orchestral support to most of "the second- and third-rate concerto composers of the Romantic dawn: Field, Kalkbrenner, Moscheles and the rest." This, however, as shown by the works themselves, is not true of Hummel's use of the orchestra in his Concertos, especially not of the first in A minor, nor is it true of Field's orchestral backing. The ineptitude and restriction were Chopin's, who seemed unable to invent anything at all telling for the orchestra while the solo part was under way, contenting himself mostly with sustained and low-placed chords to provide a background: no interesting rhythmic patterns and little spread to the texture ——— little indeed that rises above the middle range. One has only to look at the orchestral part of any Field Concerto to see the difference: the considerable use he makes of the upper note-range, the lines in counterpoint to the piano's which he gives the orchestra and the considerable rhythmic diversity he invents for accompanying figures, all providing a very much more interesting orchestral web of sound. Similarly, the orchestral part of this Concerto of Hummel's is, as has been said, an expert one. Chronologically there is a misconception here too. Hummel, though born four years earlier, could not have passed on his concerto style to Field, since the latter's first five Concertos for the instrument appeared well before any of the former's.*

Abraham calls the final movements of both Chopin Concertos "Hummelian Rondos: the F minor by Hummel out of the Mazurka, the E minor even more Hummelian and rather superficial in its charm, though with a touch of humour almost worthy of Beethoven ——— the reappearance of the principal theme a semitone flat, a 'Mistake' which is not corrected till 8 bars later." While it is indeed possible to call the last-mentioned Rondo Hummelian (there being a pointer here too to a further line of descent), it could equally well be Fieldian: it so happens that we shall find a motif essentially the same as Chopin's main thematic one and his bass pattern to it in

---

*An early Concerto in C, Op. 34, written during Hummel's classical period, and far simpler in style, was published in 1824 by Haslinger (as *Zweites* Concerto, which it could not, in any case, have been ——— the second *Grand* Concerto in B minor as well as the A minor being already in print ——— but was the second they printed). Haslinger published Hummel's little Concertino in G, Op. 73, which is entirely Mozartian in manner, in 1816, the year which saw the issue of Field's second, third and fourth Concertos.

Field works of c. 1811 and c. 1812 respectively, the first a *Rondeau* and the second the Rondo movement of a Sonata. Indeed, ideas in Hummel's first movement appear to have sparked off Chopin's first movement of the E minor Concerto and ideas from Field works his third and to have contributed, as we saw when discussing the latter's third Concerto, to his second. And as we now know, that 'mistake' in the Rondo, while it may also be nearly worthy of Beethoven, is by Chopin after Field, the same device of a semitone shift occurring in the Rondo of that composer's fourth Concerto (it was exampled when that work was discussed).

Again, concerning this same Rondo of Chopin's, Herbert Weinstock expresses the opinion that "he held his fancy in the tight reins of an inept conception of the key relationships of the classical concertos, or ––– more accurately ––– of the concertos of Gyrowetz, Hummel, and perhaps Kalkbrenner." While this gives a reason for the young Chopin's less adventurousness in form, and though Chopin went on, as would be expected of a young composer, to encompass works of far greater variety and range, I feel that his ineptitude here in much more in the orchestral handling. That he gave up his attempt at a third Concerto supports his view.

Writing about the Concertos of Chopin, Arthur Hedley says: "His only models were the fashionable concertos of Kalkbrenner, Ries, Hummel and Field, in which the orchestra is relegated to the inferior position of providing an accompaniment to the 'expressivities' and virtuosic display of the soloist." Is not, though, the expressiveness and display of the solo part a particular purpose of the Concerto as a form? Hedley's judgment, with its implied criticism of these composers' handling of the orchestra, is only in one sense true of Field who, though he gives passages to the piano which could, with advantage to the contrast, have been given instead to the orchestra, writes orchestral parts which are immensely fuller and more imaginative than Chopin's, and it is even less so of Hummel. Field's ineptness was over structure and the course of the music; Chopin's was in handling the orchestra. Hummel's grasp, in the case of the A minor Concerto at least, in which he gave us his richest music, showed an admirable balance in all respects. Hedley concludes with "He (Chopin) had had the privilege of meeting Hummel in 1828, and when he came to write his concertos the inexperienced youth naturally followed the older man more or less closely, so far as the scaffolding of the concertos was concerned." Only the scaffolding? With its neglect it is possible that Hedley might never have heard Hummel's Op. 85 in A minor, but one has to wonder if he had ever really examined it or a Field Concerto. (This is to miss, too, any Field influence in Chopin's Concertos.)

Hummel's second, third and fourth Concertos, and the posthumous last Concerto in F. Op. 127, entitled *Retour à Londres*, are by no means of the same musical quality. No. 3 in E major, Op. 110, has the title *Les Adieux de Paris.* * It is incomprehensible that the composer who wrote the expressive first in A minor could write the singularly empty third and not much less so fifth. Hummel reached a peak with Op. 85, afterwards making a sharp decline as far as the content of his music was concerned. As his decoration of his ideas became more extravagant, sometimes with passage-work running virtually from one end of the keyboard to the other (the slow movement of the F sharp minor Sonata, for instance, is sunk under the weight of this), so the ideas themselves became thinner. The themes of the fourth Concerto in A flat, in contrast to the luxuriance of their embellishment, have a particularly saccharine quality, if one excepts the more promising opening subject of the last movement. All the same, technical patterns these Concertos contain, and some thematic elements in them, still had something to say to Chopin.

The theme of the slow movement of the second Concerto in B minor. Op. 89 (published by Peters in 1820, who brought this out before Haslinger produced the first Concerto, Op. 85, in the next year), has spaciousness, if it rather lacks colour:

Though this may not have very much to say to us today, it seems probable that it was reflected, and transmuted, by Chopin in the second subject of the Allegro de Concert, which in its first and simpler statement is rhythmically extremely close to it:

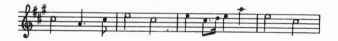

Grove's Dictionary gives Op. 110 as Rondo *Les Adieux de Paris* only, whereas this is the opus number of the full third Concerto in E.

while in its more decorated form, *p* or *f*, with Hummel's bass reproduced also, the resemblance is even more striking:

Arthur Hedley mentions one writer, unnamed, as finding an equivalent of Chopin's melody in a theme in Bellini's *I Puritani,* and who deduces an influence by the latter over the former. Hedley states a reflection in this case to be impossible, since Chopin's theme was written three years before the opera was produced. But Hummel's Concerto was written earlier, and we know that Chopin both knew and taught this work.

Likewise the next pattern, in Hummel's Rondo to this Concerto, gives a definite feeling of Chopin:

repeated from the
2nd beat of bar one

while the same movement provides:

The correspondence will be immediately evident between the last and the following example from the Allegro de Concert:

The third Concerto in E, Op. 110 (published in 1825), exhibits increasing movement over the keyboard for the solo instrument, while the ideas the work contains are among Hummel's thinnest. The slow movement especially displays an overweight of passage-work, mostly of an arpeggio, broken chord or scale basis, with the hands playing on octave apart. Not only the themes but the decorative elements lack warmth. Most of this Concerto is mere wind; only occasionally is there a more graceful or romantic moment. The theme of the Rondo, while in type supporting the idea that Hummel could have received an influence from Field, is particularly silly:

Field never wrote anything remotely as shallow as this.

Hummel's fourth Concerto in A flat, Op. 113 (pub. 1830), might strike one as a not very adept Chopin imitation did one not know the comparative dates of the two composers. Chopin had already acknowledged in his music an influence from the older composer's A minor Concerto (in the Rondo in C of 1828) and was currently doing so additionally in his E minor Concerto, written in 1830 and published in 1833. This latest Concerto of Hummel's was also to contribute its quota of influential ideas. Chopin's F minor Concerto even, composed during 1829 and 1830, contains one or two close correspondences which could point to knowledge of the Hummel work; the latter was certainly written before his own No. 2, and it is possible he might have heard it (in whole or part) during the previous year or so (it could even be at a meeting with the composer, since he was now acquainted with him). The figuration in this work has considerably more warmth, but Hummel goes to extremes in his employment of it. The next three examples will show its type: in the first movement:

(a)

(b)

and in the Finale:

(c)

followed by the
same in the major

Once can at once relate (a) to passage-work in the first movement of Chopin's F minor Concerto, while in (b) can be seen the figure Chopin uses in one of the most arresting passages in the Fantasie, the modulating one of six bars beginning:

Indeed, all the passages, (a), (b) and (c), have a Chopin-like manner and connotations.

In the first movement again, the following progression:

has the feeling of being a prior statement of a passage in the slow movement of Chopin's second Concerto, with which it has an obvious affinity:

While the passage-work in the Hummel Concerto proliferates, the form suffers and the themes and their treatment have a cloying quality, excepting this, the main subject of the last movement, the tail-phrase of which has a typically Chopin-like curl:

The content and purpose of the movement, though, do not live up to the promise of the theme. Overdecorated, the slow movement lacks colour and with it meaning.

The posthumously issued fifth Concerto in F, Op. 127, like the third, is one of Hummel's least imaginative pieces and so hardly worth considering. In it his style took a backward step. The themes are Mozartian in type, combined in the not very complicated first movement with passage-work which shows some echoes of that in Field's seventh Concerto. The slow movement is alarmingly over-weighted with figuration (basically scale passage or chromatic) for the piano, which runs 'at the quadruple' almost without inter-mission, while the last movement is a rather simple one in $\frac{3}{4}$. Haslinger had the plates ready in 1835, but the work was not issued till 1838–9, after a Cantata of Beethoven's which bore the previous plate number. Owing to its prior preparation, the Haslinger edition did not describe it as posthumous, this being added in later printings by other publishers, including one by Breitkopf of 1839 which listed it as Oeuvre posthume No. 1, other editions adhering to the Op. 127 numbering.

Thus the beautiful A minor Concerto remains an isolated master-work among Hummel's romantic output. In the Introductory Note to the 1892 Cotta Edition of the composer's works, Wilhelm Speidel, then a professor at Stuttgart Conservatoire, gives credit to

Hummel's "formal proportions," but expresses the opinion that "his works rarely reach the eminence of Mozart's, by reason alone of the overabundance of figuration and ornamentation, traits which occasionally remind us of Rossini's operatic manner (then becoming so popular), and which with Hummel often degenerate into mere superficialities, to the detriment of the intrinsic thought." The composer's slow movements suffer especially in this respect.

As has been said, the change in Hummel's style from a classical to a romantic bias came comparatively late in his works, *La Bella Capricciosa,* of which the Introduction is classical and Beethoven-like in feeling and the *Alla polacca* more romantic, being Op. 55, and the Rondo Brillant, in which the more romantic mood extends to the Introduction also, being Op. 56.

Already hinted at, here a further possibility presents itself. By the time Hummel's *La Bella Capricciosa* and Rondo Brillant appeared in 1815, pieces by Field in this style were well known, and the first five of the latter's Concertos were in print (No. 3 in 1815, Nos. 2, 3 and 4 in 1816 and No. 5 in 1817) before Hummel's first and second Concertos were published (Op. 85 in 1821 and Op. 89 shortly before it in 1820, by different publishers). Who is to say that Field's more poetic treatment of the piano did not influence the so far more prosaic Hummel who, himself a pianist of renown, would be certain to have known and very likely to have played works by the Irish composer? Indeed, this would seem to be borne out by the works mentioned and their dates. Certainly the *Alla Polacca* and the Rondo Brillant bear a Field-like cast both in themes and passage-work ——— one can mention in this connection the Rondo of Field's first Sonata (publ. 1801), the *Midi* Rondo (first version c. 1810), and the *Rondeau* of the second *Divertissement* (c. 1811).

The following two excerpts, (a) and (b), from the first movement of the A minor Concerto, with accompanying examples showing closely complementary patterning in passages in Field works, would appear to confirm a Field-Hummel link:

(a)

Hummel's development section.

Field: Rondo of Concerto No. 2.

(b)

Hummel: bravura climax passage leading to recapitulation.

Field: climax passage before last variation in the Fantasie
on Martín y Soler's Andante, Op. 3.

Hummel also, in this Concerto, particularly its last movement,
follows Field's habit of writing running passages which are partly
legato and partly staccato. The main shape of the last movement,
too ––– with its central section in which a long flowing melody is
heard mainly on the orchestra, the piano supplying accompaniment
or decoration, this being followed by the working up to a climax of
previous material ––– matches that of the Rondo of Field's second
Concerto.

As a final example, the theme of Hummel's *Rondo Brillant mêlé
d'un Thème russe*, Op. 98.* for piano and orchestra and also in a
solo version (and not only the theme of this work), has an
undeniably Fieldian ring:

*Published 1825–27.

Field met Hummel in Moscow in 1822 and the two became great friends. Not so much this, as the renown and spread of the former's works, of which Hummel must have been conscious, and the change in the latter's style occurring shortly after these began to appear and to make their mark, would suggest the possibility of an influence. Whereas Hummel altered his style from this time on, Field began to form an individual one in early works, maintaining and developing it in later.

In the final analysis it must be said that Hummel wrote a great deal of confidently constructed, often technically exacting but in the main rather dull music, with the exception of just a few works, whereas Field's music, often fumblingly put together, is shot with the constant flashing of true poetry, and it is very clear which composer had the greater feeling for the piano and thereby the more fertile influence. With Field we are conscious of greater seriousness and a greater expressiveness, despite the frequently uncomfortable frameworks into which he fits his ideas. Hummel's Rondo Brillant, Op. 56, is charming if rather long-winded; in his A minor Concerto he surpassed himself to create an isolated peak which is also a master-work of the earlier Romantic period.

9.
Field: Other Works

The remaining pieces by Field in print at one time or another comprise piano arrangements of popular tunes (the very first); three Sonatas, Op. 1, and the later Sonata in B major; three Fantasies[1]; two *Divertissements* with String Quartet (i.e. for Piano Quintet) and an A flat *Rondeau-Quintet*, with the Rondos for piano solo derived therefrom; a *Rondeau Ecossais* and a Rondoletto; a Polonaise in E flat (not the earlier mentioned and discussed *Polonaise en Rondeau* adapted from the Polacca of the third Concerto); Variations; an *Exercice modulé* (this is an extended study) and several other *Exercices;* a *Marche Triomphale;* an Introduction and Rondo (Cavatina); an Andante in E flat; a Quintet in A flat, consisting of a single movement; Waltzes for piano solo and piano duet; a *Rondeau* and other piano duet pieces; fingered Passages; two songs (?) and a vocal duet, the text lost. Also, a short *Largo* written for Madame Szymanowska remained unpublished until Cecil Hopkinson printed a photographic facsimile of the MS in his *Thematic Catalogue,* and several pieces known to have been published have remained untraced.[2] A few other pieces, presumably MSS only, mentioned by various writers, have similarly not so far been found.

Not all these (the some-time published works and the photo-printed piece) are worth examining in the light of the present discussion. The cheerful arrangements of cheerful tunes which make up the composer's earliest known compositions (*Fah Lah La* and *The Favourite Hornpipe,* to name the first two) reveal nothing pertinent to our subject or as yet any point of Fieldian originality, though the first is a piece of several pages. Works, though, among the early opus numbers show elements which apply: the first Sonata, for example (but less so the second and third), and the Fantasie, Op. 3.

The three sonatas comprising Op. 1 were first published in England in 1801. The first movement of the first Sonata (in E flat) has a classical manner and a pleasant warmth, if it exhibits repetition of phrases rather more than development. For example, one particular rhetorical phrase-ending (one might call it a phrase-interruption) recurs a number of times, no less than four of them in

---

[1] For piano; and another for Piano and Orchestra, lost, its solo version, Variations on a Russian Air, now known.

[2] A mentioned Impromptu on a Handel air is almost certainly one by Cramer on the theme.

the exposition:

This turn of phrase would seem to have found a niche in Chopin's thought and he writes this strikingly similar one in the E flat Rondo:

The second movement of this Sonata (it has only the two movements) is perhaps Field's most celebrated piece; for a long time it seems to have been his only really well-known one. Played and published separately as Rondo in E flat, it has been arranged for two pianos and was incorporated by Hamilton Harty into his *A John Field Suite* for orchestra, of which it was again the movement most frequently heard. In type it set the mood for all Field's Rondos in $\frac{2}{4}$ time, those for piano solo or piano with strings and those in the Concertos, though it, the *Midi* Rondo and that from the second *Divertissement* are better constructed than any of the composer's larger movements in the same style. (Similarly, as has been mentioned, the shorter *Polonaise en Rondeau,* in $\frac{3}{4}$, scores by reason of its greater tautness over the Polacca of the third Concerto from which it is taken.) There can be few who have not heard this Rondo or its airy theme, the sort of melody to be whistled by errand boys before 'pop' provided them with a more constant supply of easily rememberable tunes:

The movement contains several Chopin pointers, one being an example of Field's method of spinning out a link between sections or thematic ideas by taking a short cadential motif in an upward or downward course, repeating it at each step, after this fashion:

Bars 2 and 3 of this are given a repeat an octave lower, the start of this being seen in the last half-bar. An analogy can be traced between Field's method of so extending a link and the following in the first movement of Chopin's G minor Piano Trio (to give one example of his use of the same device):

Chopin repeats his 4-beat motif (also a cadential one) again, an octave higher still.

Another pattern, the basis of several bars of passage-work in the Field:

would seem to be the antecedent of one similarly founded, if wider-straddling, in the first movement of Chopin's F minor Concerto:

Leading to the final return of his theme, Field employs the triplet figuration he used in the coda of the Rondo of the first Concerto, and which provided the movement's most poetic sequence. Here it is necessary to note the bass progression and that of the right hand's lowest note in each six-semiquaver unit particularly:

We can see Chopin working to the same ground-plan in a passage from the Grande Polonaise Brillante:

Also in E flat major, below the prevailing C and B flat at the top, the right-hand under-line rises from D to A flat and returns to D (like Field's line common to his right-hand lower and left-hand upper notes), while the bottom line also follows the course of Field's, rising from B flat to F and descending again to B flat. Chopin's ostinato B flat of his left hand's upper part is there too in the Field passage: in the left hand's middle notes.

The opening of the second Sonata (Op. 1, No. 2), anticipates the piano's entry in the second Concerto, without possessing the same imagination and romanticism. It is interesting to us here only because of this foreshadowing. Field contents himself with using the same rhythmic pattern for the first three bars, in tonic, dominant seventh and tonic harmony respectively; he uses it for the first bar only in the Concerto statement. The key this time is A major.

While the first phrase of four bars is thus more matter of fact than in the later work, the poetic second one with its flowering into a rising and descending scale-based arabesque which makes the statement in the Concerto so remarkable, is missing. And though the second subject of the first movement and the bridge passage leading to it have an operatic complexion and decorative elements have begun to appear, only briefly is Field's later manner suggested. In the whole Sonata, the following phrase comes nearest to doing this and is all which might, presumably, have made any impression on Chopin:

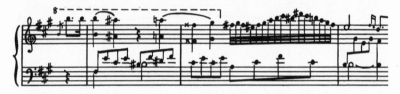

The second movement (again there are only two) is, like the first, an *Allegro vivace,* this time in $\frac{3}{4}$, and is classical in cast, with a Schubertian flavour.

The classical derivation is again obvious in the Sonata in C minor, Op. 1, No. 3, which has a C major second movement and again consists of the two movements only. Field did not give any of the four Sonatas ——— these three and the later in B major ——— more than two movements, and the intellectual shortcomings they reveal proved to be an aspect which he subsequently overcame only occasionally in his more extended pieces and never in the larger works. The most satisfactory of all the Sonatas remains the first and the best balanced and most convincing movement from them is its Rondo. The first movement of the third Sonata shows a few wider-straddling technical patterns which point to its composer's future, more-developed style, without, however, providing any specific Chopin implications. The second movement, a Rondo in $\frac{6}{8}$ marked *Allegro scherzando,* is lively if it does not show any particular originality.

Field's piano duet pieces remained on the whole less adventurous and more classical in manner than his solo works. The earliest of these, *Air Russe Varié à Quatre Mains 'How have I grieved you',* in A minor, which had a Russian publication during the first decade of the eighteen-hundreds and an English around 1811, has, however, some sprightly work for the first player if the second does not have much to do, being given an easy accompaniment. In the duet's later decorative passages for the first player, Field makes a good deal of use of the quaver/semiquaver pattern seen in the opening:

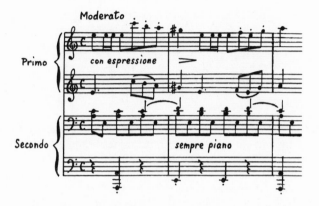

The *Divertissement avec Quatour* No. 1 in E major was first published in Russia about 1810. Without the quartet backing, this was published as a piano solo in England and Italy in 1813, under the titles in these countries respectively of *The Favourite Rondo* and *Rondeau Favori.* In 1832, in England, Field made a second version for piano solo, shorter by 49 bars, giving it then the title of *Midi* Rondo, from the twelve strokes of the *midday* bell or clock-chime heard at the end of the piece. The first edition records this as being played by a pupil of Field's, a Miss Jonas, at his concert on Wednesday May 30th, 1832, at the Great Concert Room of the Kings Theatre (question: its first performance). This, the version we know today, is generally printed as one of the Nocturnes (usually the last, to which it belongs neither in title nor in mood). The piece has clear links in character and in pianistic manner with the early Chopin Rondos like his Op. 1, that of the first Concerto, and the *Krakowiak.* The first of these would seem to owe more than a little to its opening theme:

While Chopin's first theme has, over a like polka bass, an initial rhythmic pattern in the right hand which matches that of Field's first bar:

his second melody in E major not only has the polka bass rhythm on the same foundation notes and with the same chords as Field's (with the slight difference that the latter softens his second, F sharp minor, chord with an added E, the seventh), but its line, beginning as his on B and having E as its second note, lands similarly on C sharp, F sharp, B and E in turn on the first beats of bars 2, 3 and 4 and the second beat of bar 4:

Where the classical composers would usually decorate but not change harmonically, Field, as Chopin was habitually to do, subtly varies the complexion of his theme at its reappearances: by altering its line in the second bar to:

and by changing the bass first in bar 2 and then in bar 3, making these read at the second appearance of the theme:

and at the third

Chopin uses the polka bass again in the Finale of the Trio in G minor, where the main theme has a decidedly Fieldian character, linking with both the opening subject of Chopin's own Rondo of the E minor Concerto and a motif in the *Rondeau* of Field's second *Divertissement* to be seen later.

Another bass pattern appearing in the *Midi* Rondo:

has a nearly identical twin in this one in Chopin's Nocturne in B major, Op. 32, No. 1:

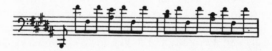

We shall shortly see Field using a similar bass, in a passage which is again in B major, when we come to the Fantasie, Op. 3. In taking over types of basses from Field, Chopin absorbed also their variants, adding further variations of his own to their patterns. For example, the more convoluted bass supporting the main theme in the Barcarole is still derived from the earlier composer's waving Nocturne accompaniments.

The *Divertissement avec Quatour* No. 2 in A, which appeared in 1811, consists of a *Pastorale et Rondeau*, the *Pastorale,* as previously stated, being the original version of Nocturne No. 8 in A major, longer by 34 bars, and the *Rondeau* being the same (or very nearly — — — a little more about this later) as the Rondo (*Favori*) No. 2. The *Pastorale* has more, and more varied, decorative passage-work for the piano then the Nocturne (length partly accounts for this) and a variations aspect missing in the latter. The *Rondeau,* while not so arresting in theme as the *Midi* Rondo, is a charming piece, with Chopin implications in its elements and figuration. It would seem also to have some links with Hummel's Rondo Brillant in the same key. Its main subject is:

while the following is typical of the passage-work it contains:

Light in mood, maybe, but with twists in its line and an elegant manner which both to the ear and under the fingers convey an impression of Chopin. And indeed, on coming across the next passage, one wonders whether the first subject of his Rondo in the E minor Concerto may not owe something (or even its existence) to it. The rhythmic patterns of both composers' first bars are the same (two quavers and a crotchet) and, like Field's, Chopin's crotchet of the second beat falls on G sharp, being likewise tied over to the first note of the next bar, which similarly is given more movement through the addition of semiquavers.

Too, this phrase of Field's and Chopin's theme are both in E major. As the Chopin motif will be given a little further on, I am not setting it out here.

A figure which appears in the Rondo of Field's sixth Concerto and the coda of the Finale of Chopin's B minor Sonata has an earlier and simpler airing in the *Rondeau* of the *Divertissement*.

Some of Field's best-shaped pieces are here in these earlier and smaller 'semi-concerto' movements (though the *Rondo Favori* No. I is less shapely than its reconstruction as the *Midi* Rondo); in the longer he was taxed beyond his ability concerning structure.

Field's *Fantasie sur l'Andante de V. Martín y Soler,* Op. 3*
(published 1812, in Leipzig) contains a good deal that anticipates
Chopin, particularly in its decorative figures involving unequal
numbers of notes and in a beautiful, rhapsodic first variation ———
the work having the form of a short introduction followed by a
statement of the theme which is given a good deal of delicate
embellishment and a cadenza as climax, followed in turn by five
variations. Apart from an effective presentation of the pensive theme
and the maintained interest of the first variation, the piece does not
hang together very well, lacking, for one thing, enterprise in
modulation. Field attempts to give some to the second variation in E
major, if not very comfortably, but is soon moving back to the basic
key of A major, after which the remaining three variations hug this
key, and the initial shape of the theme-motif is kept as the basis for
each (Field, though he adds embellishments in the course of a
variation and makes the fourth a *bravura* one with bustling background runs in demi-semiquavers, never thinks of altering this motif
rhythmically, turning it upside down, or putting a variation into the
minor). The piece has a sensitive atmosphere, largely by reason of
the pianistic nature of its decorative patterns and an awakening
romantic sonority, the latter especially evident in the first variation,
but, as with other of Field's longer pieces, one is conscious of his
inability to give it a convincingly balanced shape.

One would like to quote the whole 34 bars of the first variation,
but two passages may suffice: bars 5½—10:

and bars 26—29, where the similarity of the bass to those (also in B
major) exampled earlier from the *Midi* Rondo and Chopin's

* Two versions. Theme *Guarda mi un poco,* from the opera *La Scuola
dei Maritati.*

Nocturne Op. 32, No. 1, may be noted:

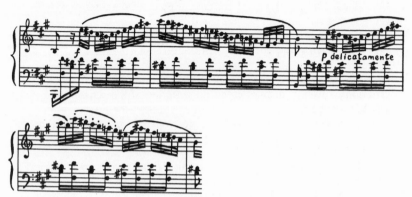

While the former has a distinct affinity with several of the passages in Chopin's Polonaise-Fantasie (on either side of the B major section), the latter must inevitably remind us again, by reason of its key, length, general contour and repeat of phrase, of the passage in the slow movement of his E minor Concerto, beginning:

This was quoted more fully earlier, when Field's third Concerto was being discussed.

As a characteristic example of the latter's arabesque figures in the *Fantasie*, the following may be given:

In what may be presumed to be Chopin's very first Nocturne, in C minor (its opening phrase the same as that of *Charlie is my Darling*), which remained unpublished until the middle of the present century, we find him writing a comparable figure:

Field did not keep up the use of opus numbers beyond this *Fantasie* and, as will have been noticed, they signified little. At least six works were published between Op. 1 and Op. 3 and no Op. 2 is traceable.

The fourth Sonata in B major was published about the same time as the *Fantasie* (c. 1812). It is hardly an efficient or distinguished example of sonata writing (there are again only two movements, the second the more extended), but it does contain patterns which anticipate Chopin, these being mostly turns of phrase, embellishments and nocturne-like basses such as we have already seen in other works. A new bass pattern, however, appears in its Rondo, being the one which Chopin uses beneath his main theme in the Rondo of the first Concerto. The following example shows the pattern as it appears in Field's movement:

and this its use in Chopin's:

Another Rondo, in A flat, comes, in its first form of a *Rondeau-Quintet* (Piano and String Quartet), within the group of works published in or about 1812. In the Quintet the *Rondeau*, marked *Allegro vivace,* was introduced by an *Andantino* of eight bars which was omitted from the piano solo version (1817). The theme, if less interesting than that of the *Midi* Rondo, is characteristic of Field's manner in this type of movement, bearing some resemblance to the subject of the Rondo of the first Concerto and, if more widely circled round, a suggestion as did that subject of the motif of the first bar of Chopin's E flat Rondo. The essential notes are asterisked in the example. (One can continue to trace a line through Field's Rondos in this style to Chopin's earlier, though the closeness of details may be in this case less discernable.)

The piece itself belongs to a number which show rather more confidence in the shaping, though it gets bogged down in tonic and dominant seventh harmony towards the end. Pianistic details and some of the passages of working-out are this time rather more interesting than the thematic basis, and the following shows Field's inventiveness in giving a new complexion to a chromatic passage:

Liszt was later to use this variety of chromatic double-stepping, in, for example, *Au bord d'une source* (upwards) and in this from the fifth of his *6 Chants Polonais* (transcriptions for piano of Chopin songs):

while Chopin, writing this in the E flat Rondo:

and giving the device this form in the *Bolero*:

uses it upwards towards the end of the 'Revolutionary' Étude, in the bass:

Field thought of just about everything when it came to coaxing new effects and technical patterns with a romantic colouring from the piano, and though others, notably Chopin and Liszt, amplified these and wove them into more watertight structures, it waited for Ravel and Debussy, particularly the latter, to find still newer patterns and sonorities and so give keyboard music its next big step forward.

While aspects of charm and vitality show in Field's pieces for piano duet, their more classical basis in general has been mentioned. In having to provide a texture involving two players the composer seems on the whole to have found himself restricted in regard to the addition of decorative effects (the earliest duet remains the most free in this respect), and the second player has always a noticeably simple part. The *Andante à Quatre Mains,* in C minor (published in 1811), has a pensive melancholy and the *Grande Valse à Quatre Mains* in A major (1812—13) possesses liveliness, without either revealing any particular inventiveness. *La Danse des Ours* (*Bears' Dance*), in E flat (1811 again), is more interesting, both for its outlay and, with a theme which falls and then rises, its suggestion of Field's Nocturne mood:

The lower part (again simple) is, however, by W. Aumann, Field presumably approving. Heinrich Dessauer in his book (1912) printed a solo version in C with some differences (of phrase and ending).

The short Polonaise in E flat (c. 1812—13) adds to a Weber-like theme decorative passage-work characteristic of its composer, of which the following is an example:

An analogy can be traced between this and patterning similarly convoluted and descending which Chopin writes in the Rondo in E flat:

The *Air du Bon Roi Varié* (Theme of Henry IVth of France), in A minor (publ. 1812–13), the *Air Avec Variations, 'Since then I'm Doomed,'* in C major (an 1818 printing known, but two much earlier mentioned), and the *Chanson Russe Variée, 'My dear bosom Friend,'* in D minor (c. 1818), are all nearer Dussek in style than the more poetic manner we have learned to expect from the composer. With so little known of the dates of composition of Field's works, it is possible that all are, like the second, earlier than their publication dates suggest. While Field's grounding in the classical tradition was apt to take over at such times as he was less inspired towards the creation of new sonorities (the 'Cavatina,' for example, mixes the romantic and classical approaches), we may remember that the first movement of the second Concerto (or a good part of it), with its very different complexion, was in existence by 1811 and that by 1818 the first six of the Nocturnes, with their blend of poetry and nostalgia, and the first five Concertos were in print. The last-named set of variations especially is pianistic if Field's range is noticeably less extended in all these works. To give the opening of the variation which is perhaps the most interesting of the seven the *Chanson Russe Variée* contains:

Coming in between these last-named in publication (i.e. between the first and the last two), but more pertinent to our subject, is the *Air Russe Favori Varié 'Kamarinskaya,'* in B flat (1813–14). The setting out of the well-known theme is less imaginative and less important than the technical variations accorded it. Field gives us not a series of variations in the usual sense, but a number of varying technical patterns of increasing difficulty round the thematic line before returning for a finish to the quiet and simple introductory phrase with which he began the piece. For the last of these patterns, at the point of greatest excitement, he presents this highly acrobatic one:

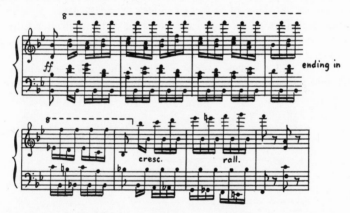

Shades of Liszt! And the very basis of Chopin's third variation of the *Là ci darem* Variations, also in B flat:

Along with other of Chopin's most arresting and seemingly individual patterns, such as that which forms the basis of the 'Winter Wind' Étude, this proves to have been Field's in the first place ––– more than thirteen years earlier.

The *Rondeau Ecossais* on the theme '*Speed the Plough*' (also

1813–14) hardly contains anything which applies to our subject. The E flat Rondo (*Polonaise en Rondeau,* 1816) emphatically does, but being a shorter version of the Polacca of the third Concerto, it has been discussed in the section devoted to the Concertos.

In 1816 Field published an *Exercice modulé dans tous les tons majeurs et mineurs.* Beginning in C major, this proceeds as its title says to modulate through all the major and minor keys and, hardly described by the word 'exercise,' is in reality a sizeable study. Its rushing semiquavers are at first played by the right hand over sustained widespread chords in the left hand until both hands share in the semiquaver motion.* The piece might well have helped Chopin formulate the idea of writing Preludes in all the keys, as well as encouraged the modulatory aspect of some of the individual Etudes, for example, the first of Op. 10. Hearing the Field, one is conscious of being close to Chopin's territory. Here are five patterns from the *Exercice*, which ranges widely over the keyboard, Field outdoing Chopin in inventing varied-length note-patterns which by crossing oppose the basic four-semiquaver groups (as (a) and (e)):

---

* In another version Field gave the L. H. semiquavers at the start.

It may not be generally known that Hummel, before Chopin, wrote a set of 24 short Preludes, Op. 57, in all the major and minor keys. Musically, though, they do not suggest Chopin, but are classical in style, and all are brief, some being single sentences of a few bars only in length.

Imaginably dating from about the time of the *Exercice modulé* (perhaps earlier in view of their numbering) are the *Exercices* No. 1 in C, *'Deux voix d'inégale valeur dans une main"* (the right hand), and No. 2 in A flat *pour la main gauche* (really Études with the sort of musical basis which Chopin's have). No. 1 shows further use of figuration to be found in the first movement of the fourth Concerto (the latter publ. 1816):

while the style and passage-work displayed by No. 2 have clear Chopin connotations:

The *Exercices* were published in Russia in a Collection of *Études et exercices pour le piano*, though I have no date(s).

The year 1816 also saw the publication of Field's *Quintetto* in A flat. The Quintet consists of a single movement, being rather like an extended pastorale or nocturne, and is more truly quintet writing and less like a piano work with string quartet accompaniment than the earlier *Divertissements,* though one should except here the *Pastorale* of the *Divertissement* No. 2, which similarly shows a greater sharing out of its content. Field's manner anticipating Chopin is here well to the fore, the piece's fault being again a sense of restriction in the direction of the music, the mood and felicity of many of the details outweighing this in success. The warm opening is a particularly good example of the composer's romantic manner:

with considerable overtones of Chopin in its mood, as in the later
variaton and decoration given to its line. The piano, for example,
gives the end of the first phrase a new complexion by turning it in
this fashion:

one of this instrument's typical decorative passages being:

In a later statement the last is given further impetus by means of
semiquaver triplets and demi-semiquavers, its second bar, for
example, being:

All of these lines, the calm and the more fleet, have the elegance
which has come to be regarded as a hall-mark of Chopin. Though
this music has a simpler texture than much of his, one can think of
only two composers likely to have written it: Field and Chopin. This
final extract, from a point of climax in the movement, exemplifies
this aspect in terms which unmistakably point forward to the music
of the later composer:

In this next example Chopin is to be found using the same figuration in the Rondo in C minor, Op. 1:

Field did not, apparently, consider adding other movements to this isolated one to make a larger chamber work. Difficulties over structure may have deterred him, and we are left with a piece more important in its mood and details than in the sum of its parts, the title of Quintet seeming rather grandiose for its brevity. Despite the warmth and charm of its manner, one can imagine the members of an audience, after hearing it, looking at each other and querying "Is that all there is?" The highly original poetic quality of its writing make it worthy of our consideration in a way which the course and extent of the music do not. As with the other works for piano and strings, Field made a piano solo version of this movement, with the marking *Andante espressivo*, though it remained unpublished.

The *Nouvelle Fantasie sur le motif de la Polonaise 'Ah Quel Dommage'* (1816), in G major, the theme from Boildeau's opera *Le Caliph de Baghdad*, and the *Nouvelle Fantasie* in G (published in 1833), both having a variations-form basis, contain characteristic decorative elements, the later and simpler (a theme and four variations) being the more interesting and confidently shaped. The former, for example, contains a good deal of luxuriant and some technically exacting passage-work, while being at the same time singularly undirected harmonically and in shape.

The *Rondeau* No. 2 in A (1817), in some editions Rondo *Favori* No. 2 (No. 1 being the earlier version of the *Midi* Rondo) is a later printing as a piano solo of the *Rondeau* from the second *Divertissement* with small alterations. For example, the melodic line of the opening has been changed (and the bass chords adjusted) to:

which at first makes one think it a different piece until one finds
that it is otherwise virtually the same. The dedication is to the same
person: Comtesse d'Orloff Tschemensky. To be noted here is the
shape of the second part of the motif:

which along with its slightly different shaping in the *Rondeau* of the
Divertissement:

can be equated with the shape of Chopin's motif involving the same
degrees of the scale in his E flat Rondo:

Asterisks mark the essential notes in each example. Field having used
this turn of phrase ——— of a curve round the 3rd, 6th, 5th, 4th and
2nd notes of the scale, and especially the portion falling from the
6th to the 2nd ——— in the themes of three Rondos, Chopin's motif
can now be seen to have links with all of these: besides the two
versions of this A major subject, that of the Rondo of the first
Concerto (where the five notes appear in direct order), and also, as
has been shown, that of the A flat Rondo (*Rondeau-Quintet*), where
the series is outlined more loosely and the penultimate (4th) degree
omitted.

The piano duet, *Rondeau à Quatre Mains,* in G major (1819), has
vitality along with a classical cast, Field's imagination, as has been
said, appearing more restricted in the pieces for two players. They
were probably written to fill a need, when the occasion required
something for pupils to play or perform together, and as such were
utility pieces.

The Six Dances (1820), for piano solo, are similarly less
characteristic, being rather like Beethoven's German Dances and

Écossaises with a touch of Schubert's waltz-style. They are lively, but their piano writing is of a blunter description and they would fit quite well into a classical programme. They comprise three Waltzes with Trios, two Quadrilles and an Anglaise.

The *Exercice Nouveau* (publ. 1821–22) and the *Nouvel Exercice* No. 2 (1822), both in C major, if quite extensive are less important than the Exercices discussed earlier.

The Fantasie for Piano and Orchestra, in A minor (written in 1823), on a Russian theme, the favourite air of Field's friend N.P., and its solo version, Variations on the Russian Air *In the Garden? In the Vegetable Plot?*,* were published in Russia during the 1820s. The orchestral parts being at present lost while one would like to know details of the balance between the solo part and orchestra, the interplay of the material and textural interweaving, the work can only be mentioned as a solo.

The theme bears a not unfamiliar complexion of a gentle Russian melancholy:

the piece, which works up to some lively climax material, having a free variation, ternary basic form with a development aspect to the more brilliant central section, in which key contrasts play their part. Characteristic technical and decorative patterns occur, involving effects, delicate and *bravura*, such as we have seen in the Concertos. The following may be of interest for the appearance of a reminder of Field's (and Chopin's) ' raindrops ' device in note-pairs in the bass with a reflection of the first bar of the theme in the major below it, the latter a type of derivative pattern-making less usual for the composer:

*The Andante with Variations which Grattan Flood mentions Field as having played at the Haydn Centenary Concert in London on March 21st, 1832, could perhaps be this work.

The Rondoletto in E flat (publ. 1831), a Rondo with Tarantelle overtones, has subtleties in line and harmony and is tautly constructed in a way which makes it incomprehensible that the same composer could have written the singularly fumbling Rondo of the fourth Sonata. The theme shows an affinity with other previous Field Rondo themes:

while the following displays a technical pattern

which Chopin used in the Bolero (written two years later):

The *Sehnsüchts-Walzer*, Cecil Hopkinson tells us, had its first known printing in 1845. In giving this date, he states that it had a likely but untraceable printing much earlier. It is a short but elegant, completely pianistic and captivating little waltz. The light-hearted mood which nevertheless retained an aspect of superficiality in some of Field's Rondo themes (in that of the A flat Rondo but not the *Midi* Rondo, and those of the Rondos of the fifth and sixth Concertos but not of the second, e.g.), receives here an absolute and transforming polish. The Waltz has gaiety, sensitivity in every turn of phrase, and tenderness. It is a romantic gem, and a worthy forerunner to the best of Chopin's. Oh, for a volume of such waltzes from Field, instead of one perfect example!* Its theme in full (a) and its wistful final phrase (b) need imperatively to be quoted.

*Of the three Waltzes and two Quadrilles in waltz-time in the Six Dances, none match this in quality, though, while I lack details, Probst published a Selection of *Mödetanze* which may have contained extra pieces of the type.

So exquisitely turned is this small piece that a note could not be altered or its brief duration changed without harming it; one might like more but would dread any addition ——— the only (and satisfying) response therefore being to play or hear it again. Not at present in print, it was published for a time with another less interesting Waltz in E, called *Frühlings-Walzer,* until that was subsequently found to be by Weber. It would not be too much to say that in this aspect of his style Field, in this little Waltz, reached full maturity, which makes me inclined to place it as coming later rather than earlier among his compositions, probably around the time of writing of the ' waltz-mazurka ' Rondo of the seventh Concerto ——— but that is conjecture only, and while he was entirely happy in shaping the *Sehnsüchts-Walzer,* he could not control the material of the Rondo in the same way.

An Andante (Inédit) in E flat was published in Russia in 1852, and has fairly recently come to light again. Cecil Hopkinson mentions knowledge of one edition of this and hearing about another, without at the time being able to trace a copy of either. The piece contains many turns of phrase and decorative passages giving a feeling of Chopin ——— one, for instance, like the falling figure in the latter's Grande Polonaise Brillante:

While once more revealing aspects of similarity between the two composers' styles, it is unlikely the piece was written before the Polonaise and it could show points of a reverse influence. Whether Chopin ever heard it is entirely conjectural.

It is perhaps appropriate that the final work to be examined should be the *Introduction and Rondo on Blewitt's Celebrated Cavatina 'Reviens! Reviens!'* first printed in England in 1832, and sometimes published simply as *Cavatina,* with the subtitle *'Reviens! Reviens!'* and no mention of the derivation of the theme.

In the Introduction we are back, with considerable chromatic harmony, in the territory of Field's and Chopin's Nocturnes, with the aroma of Chopin stronger than ever:

the end of Field's first phrase of eight bars being:

The end of Chopin's first phrase in the Andante Spianato describes the same outline (bracketed in the last example):

Above a left hand which for five bars remains the same, Field gives
the first repeat of the theme this variation:

and the second this:

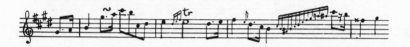

Chromatic passing notes in the left hand patterns and chromatic
chord changes add to the nostalgic mood of the section, a
characteristic progression being:

The opening *Adagio* is the more redolent with atmosphere. The
Rondo theme springs from the *Cavatina* melody of this
Introduction, compressed into:

In this second and longer part of the work passages of romantic
colouring alternate with sections showing a more classical approach.
Here the passages of *volante* semiquavers which finish off each of the
two halves into which the Rondo roughly falls most show Field's
particular romanticism, while displaying once more his very personal
handling of keyboard figuration ——— the links being again
unmistakable with similar passages in Chopin, which exhibit the
same sort of refinement and melodic quality in their convolutions

and which require the same sort of finger dexterity. The first passage remaining quiet, *pp* and *p,* and the second allowed to rise to *f* at the end, the running patterns occupy 18 and 16 bars respectively. Here are two bars from the first (a) and the start of the second (b):

In the first of these passages Field varies his polka bass by sometimes filling up the fourth quaver of each half bar and sometimes writing chords on each of the four beats; in the second he keeps the bass pattern throughout.

One does not have to look far to find Chopin writing passages in the same manner, for example, in the A flat Polonaise, Op. 53 (in the section beginning in G major before the return of the main theme), and in this from the Impromptu in F sharp, Op. 36:

The Chopin is the more serious in mood, but the passages are nevertheless of the same lineage.

Remaining pieces not touched on in this discussion of Field's other works are *The Two Favourite Slave Dances in Blackbeard*; his arrangement for piano of Pleyel's Concertante in F major; *Marche Triomphale* in E flat, its theme a little like the main subject of the first movement of the first Concerto (simple but charming);

88 Passages (from the Concertos and other pieces) fingered by the composer; and a short chordal *Largo* written for Madame Szymanowska, which could be a first thought for the opening theme of the seventh Concerto. The more telling mood of the last having already been embraced in the discussion of the Concerto, the original pieces here are of a description or slightness such as to contribute little or nothing to the subject in hand. Words were attached to the melodies of two of the Nocturnes, Nos. 1 and 5, and these published as songs, if it is not quite certain Field arranged them.* Published first in an Italian edition of 1825, a Petrarch Sonnet was fitted to No. 1 (or the Nocturne adapted to fit the Sonnet), and an Ode by d'Ippolito Pindemonte to No. 5. The keys were changed to B flat and F majors respectively. The themes of these works, including the piano and vocal outlay of the two songs, can be found in Cecil Hopkinson's *Thematic Catalogue* of the composer's works, in which he lists a number of other pieces either known to have been published or mentioned by various writers without there being any record of their content. These (apart from one or two now known) are the previously-mentioned Nocturne, *Dernière Pensée*; a *Pastorale* (according to the MS of Field's pupil Reinhardt); *Logie of Buchan* Rondo; *Slave, Bear the Sparkling Goblet Round; Go to the Devil and Shake Yourself;* and a song (vocal duet) *The Maid of Valdarno.* Copies or MSS of these may, of course, yet be found, and also of other works, even the spoken-of eighth Concerto of 1835, if not very likely, it being not impossible that this exists. While works not in print during Chopin's lifetime, and with which it is merely conjectural whether he could have come into contact (through MS or hearing), do not affect the main theme of this book, any afterwards discovered or printed, including lost works turning up and possible unknown still to be found, could perhaps form the subject of a later study and also supply interesting performing pieces if their content should be sufficiently balanced.

Outside the popular tunes which he arranged for his first pieces, very little ' Irishness ' seems evident in Field's music. The possibility of one or two of his melodies having Irish folk-tune counterparts has been suggested to me, but I have failed to find the latter. The only figure which might be described as having this complexion is the two note one of ♫. of which he makes use, for example, in the *Pastorale* of the second *Divertissement* and the *Grande Pastorale*

---

* While the second edition (German) bears a dedication and ascribes them to him, the first states the music *adattata sopra* a Nocturne for Piano of Field (a), and over the *motivo* of a Nocturne (b).

(and the Nocturnes Nos. 8 and 17 derived from them). But this pattern is equally Scottish: a characteristic element in so many Scottish tunes, it is a feature of the melody *Within a mile of Edinburgh town* on which he bases the slow movement of the first Concerto.

'*Reviens! Reviens!*' ——— Return! Return! ——— but to the composer this time. More needs knowing of Field (and more has begun to be known since this book was started); known not always for the satisfaction to be obtained from his music, but for the importance of his pianistic innovations and the position he rightly occupies at the head of the Romantic movement in musical composition, a position which has for too long been denied him.

He, like Chopin, was primarily a writer for the pianoforte, though he had a far more developed sense of other instruments and of the orchestra than the latter. But, again like Chopin, he never wrote for orchestra alone and left no solo work for violin, cello or any other instrument. The single song definitely his is now untraceable. Chopin extended his range to write effectively for the cello, if not equally comfortably in every work involving it, but not for the violin and his one Trio, in G minor, the second earliest of his chamber works, is an unhappy example of the form, with that instrument especially being used with singular lack of imagination. His songs ——— apart from the final one, a little masterpiece of melancholy and expressiveness ——— are not among the most significant part of his output.

While it is true to say that the piano music of Chopin was the finest flowering of the Romantic period, it is not true to call him "The most truly original of all composers."[1] or "one of the great originators."[2] Like Keats, who took so much from Barnes, Chopin was a considerable acquirer of elements from earlier composers sympathetic to him. Another of his favourite works, according to Niecks, was the Concerto in E minor by Moscheles, and one wonders what patterns from it may perhaps have reappeared in his music. Again, like Keats in poetry, he wove a complete, full-bodied and entirely satisfactory musical means of expression from and around these elements. In this, and far less in the elements themselves, lies his originality, this having been the view of Niecks, who concluded that Chopin was original by what he made of "the commixture of

[1] *Men of Music.*
[2] Centenary article in the *Musical Times.*

known elements:" that is, that acquisition and evolvement contributed to making his so significant an art. Hummel took a considerable time to reach (or change over to) a full romantic expressiveness, then lost this again. Field reached this after a very few works and was undoubtedly the originator, if his unequal command of structure led to the bulk of his music being dropped from favour.

This acquisition of Chopin's, so extensive in its scope, does not, in my opinion, reduce his stature as a composer, but shifts the emphasis ——— though it is not, incidentally, considered today to be a point in a composer's favour for him markedly to reflect another, a personal slant in his colouring and methods being considered a necessity before it is accounted that he has 'found himself' and has something original to say. Here Chopin's increased complexity set against Field's generally simpler textures and his far keener ear for the balanced course of the music would constitute his originality, though, with Field's music unknown, all the colouring and musical elements would also (as they have been) be considered his creation alone.

Even in Field's own time other musicians were aware of his varying comfort in his forms. Chopin, as has been mentioned, added his own embellishments when playing the Nocturnes (this could be, of course, for the purpose of trying his hand at similar) and Liszt, while professing his admiration of their manner and newness in his Essay to his first edition of them (of six, extended gradually to eighteen), cut a salient silence of three beats out of No. 7 and drastically shortened and made alterations of line to No. 17.* Later Busoni prepared them with his own ornamentation, but unlike Liszt's edition, these were never published. The Nocturnes, it may be said, need this treatment less than various other works, especially the larger (here Fétis' opinion of the seventh Concerto has been quoted), and No. 17 is emphatically one of those which do not require it. From Liszt's Essay it seems likely that he was responsible for the inclusion of the *Midi* Rondo among the Nocturnes, the composer never having described it as such.

It is possible that Chopin did not know all Field's works which were in circulation during his lifetime. It is unlikely that, finding the

*While generally acknowledged to be Liszt's own version, there could be a bare possibility this was Field's, since he found it difficult to make definitive forms of so many works, giving them so much alteration. The piece appeared in this form in no other edition, however, that of Liszt containing it being c. 1868, and is far more likely to be his reshaping after Field's death; the altered bass of the opening is much more like Liszt than Field. As mentioned earlier, Field made a very short version which was never published.

latter's Nocturnes and Concertos evoked in him a personal and musical response, he would be uninterested in whatever the earlier composer had written. One can, indeed, point to individual works he must have known: the *Rondo Favori* No. 1 and that from the second *Divertissement,* and the *Air Russe Favori Varié 'Kamarinskaya,'* for example, among the other works of Field.

Undoubtedly Chopin breathed the very spirit of the Romantic era, in music exhibiting the refinement of elegance and dignity and a particular integrity, and was undeniably the greater composer, in the strength and completeness of his works. But Field began all this, and it was on his foundation that Chopin built: not only the essence which he distilled of poetic feeling and sound, but the actual patterns and devices which he invented and which Chopin used even in his latest works. (While Field could never have planned, to name just one work, a piece as complex as the Barcarole, or carried it through with the same assurance and finality, that piece owes more than a little to his innovations, from its nocturne bass and floating melody to its final filagree passage.) Had Field possessed that extra facet of the ability more regularly to cast his ideas in suitable and balanced moulds, who knows what position he might not now occupy in our estimation, instead of having been for so long very nearly forgotten. Or how much less a figure Chopin might have proved had not Field's entirely personal aroma been at hand to fire his imagination.

For too long there has been a missing link in the chain of developing pianistic moods and devices which led up to the music of Chopin, giving rise to the supposition by so many, and so many writers, that he was the sole originator, whereas he was to a far greater degree than is generally thought possible the harvester and developer. It is time that it is finally acknowledged, beyond any doubt at all, that the composer who supplied that link ––– in music often fumbling and incomplete in realization but great in potential and rich in the achievement of new sonorities and decorative effects, langour and gracefulness, which came directly from the instrument and which for so long have indicated to us only Chopin ––– was John Field, the first poet of the piano.

List of Field's works
with dates of their first publication.

For Piano Solo except where otherwise indicated.

	date:
Fah Lah La (A major)	circa 1795 (England)
The Favourite Hornpipe (of *Signora del Caro*) *with variations* (A major)	c. 1795–96 (England)
Air Avec Variations 'Since Then I'm Doomed' (C major)	Untraced English publications of 1795 and 1801 mentioned; first known 1818 (Germany)
The Two Favourite Slave Dances in Blackbeard (G. major)	1798 (England)
Three Sonatas, Op. I No.I in E flat; No. 2 in A major No.3 in C minor	1801 (England)
Pleyel's Concertante in F major arranged for Piano by Field	1801 (England)
Piano Duet: *Air Russe Varié, à Quatre Mains 'How have I grieved you'* (A minor)	1808 (Russia)
Divertissement avec Quatour No. 1 in E major (the *Rondo Favori* No. 1 is a Piano Solo version of this work, and the *Midi* Rondo a recast shorter version of 1832)	c. 1810 (Russia)
Piano Duet: *Andante à Quatre Mains* (C minor)	1810 (Russia)
Piano Duet: *La Danse des Ours* (E flat)	1811 (Russia)
Divertissement avec Quatour No. 2 in A – – – *Pastorale et Rondeau*	1811 (Russia)
Fantasie sur l'Andante de V. Martín y Soler, Op. 3 (A major)	1812 (Germany)
Marche Triomphale (E flat)	1812 (Russia)
Sonata No. 4 in B major	c. 1812 (Russia)
Rondeau in A flat for Piano with String Quartet accompaniment (*Rondeau-Quintet*) – – – Andantino and Allegro vivace (solo version with 8 bars Andantino Introduction omitted published 1817)	c. 1812 (Russia)
Piano Duet: *Grande Valse à Quatre Mains* (A major)	c. 1812–13 (Russia)
Air du Bon Roi (Henri IV) Varié (A Minor)	c. 1812–13 (Russia)
Polonaise in E flat	{ c. 1812–13 (Russia) { c. 1813 (England)
Rondo Favori No. 1 (Piano Solo version of 1st Divertissement (E major)	1813 (Italy and England)

Air Russe Favori Varié 'Kamarinskaya' (B flat)	c. 1813–14 (Russia)
Rondo Ecossais 'Speed the Plough' (B flat) (B major)	{ c. 1813 (England) { c. 1813–14 (Russia) 1814 (Germany)
Three Romances *Pastorale* from *Divertissement* No. 2 in shorter Nocturne form (A major);* 1st Nocturne in E flat; 2nd Nocturne in C minor with some differences	1814 (Germany)
Three Nocturnes No. 1 in E flat; No. 2 in C minor; No. 3 in A flat	1814 (Germany)
Piano Concerto No. 1 in E flat	1815 (Germany)
Piano Concerto No. 2 in A flat	1815 (Germany)
Piano Concerto No. 3 in E flat	1816 (Germany)
Piano Concerto No. 4 in E flat	1816 (Germany)
Rondeau in E flat (*Polonaise en Rondeau*) (shorter Piano Solo version of the Polacca from the 3rd Concerto)	1816 (Germany)
Romance in E flat (same as Nocturne No. 9)	1816 (Germany)
Exercice modulé dans tous les tons majeurs et mineurs (C major)	1816 (Germany)
Exercice No. 1 in C (R.H. passage-work) *Exercice* No. 2 in A flat (L.H. passage-work)	––– (Russia) question; c. 1816
Quintetto in A flat, Piano and Strings	1816 (Germany)
Nouvelle Fantasie sur le motif de la Polonaise 'Ah Quel Dommage' (G major)	1816 (Germany)
Nocturne No. 4 in A major	{ c. 1818–17 (Russia) { 1817 (Germany
Nocturne No. 5 in B flat	{ c. 1816–17 (Russia) { 1817 (Germany)
Nocturne No. 6 in F major (same as the slow movement of Concerto No. 6, with the key changed from E major to F)	{ c. 1816–17 (Russia, and { in a French magazine
Rondeau (sometimes *Rondo Favori*) No. 2 (*Rondeau* from 2nd *Divertissement*, for Piano Solo with slight differences) (A major)	1817 (Russia)
Rondo in A flat (Piano Solo version of *Rondeau-Quintet* with 8 bars Introduction omitted)	1817 (England)
Piano Concerto No. 5 in C, *L'Incendie par l'Orage*	1817 (Russia and Germany)
Chanson Russe Variée 'My dear, bosom Friend' (D minor)	{ c. 1818 (Russia) { c. 1818 (Germany, two publishers)

* Nocturne No. 8 in Peters Edition.

Piano Duet: *Rondeau à Quatre Mains* (G major) — 1818 (Germany, two publishers)

Six Dances — 1820 (England)

Vocal Duet: *The Maid of Valdarno,** words by W. F. Collard (content unknown) — 1821 (England)

Exercice nouveau (C major) — { c. 1821–22 (Russia) / 1822 (Germany) }

Nocturne No. 7 in C — { c. 1821–22 (Russia) / 1822 (Germany) }

Nocturne No. 8 in E minor (No. 10 in Peters Edition) — { c. 1821–22 (Russia) / 1822 (Germany) }

Nouvel exercice No. 2 (C major) — 1823 (Germany)

Piano Concerto No. 6 in C — 1823 (Russia and Germany)

Fantasie for Piano and Orchestra on an *Air Favorit* of Field's friend N. P. (A minor)

Variations on the Russian Air *In the Garden? In the Vegetable Plot?* (version for Piano Solo) — during 1820s (Russia)

Two Songs, to Nocturnes Nos. 1 and 5 — 1825 (Italy)
    1. *Levommi il mio pensier* (Petrarch)
    2. *Melanconia* (Pindemonte)
    (question: Field's arrangement, the 2nd edition, German, but not the first, ascribing this to him.)

Rondoletto in E flat — 1831 (France and England)

Introduction and Rondo on Blewitt's Celebrated Cavatina 'Reviens! Reviens!' (E major) — 1832 (England)

Grande Pastorale in E, Piano and String Quartet (Nocturne No. 17 is a solo version of this) — 1832 (England)

Midi Rondo (Rondo 'Twelve o'Clock') (recast shorter version of *Rondo Favori* No. 1) (E major) — 1832 (England)

Nocturne, *The Troubadour* (C major) — c. 1832 (England)

Nocturne No. II in E flat — 1833 (Germany)

Nouvelle Fantasie (G major) — { 1833 (Germany and France / 1833–34 (England) }

Piano Concerto No. 7 in C minor — 1833 (Germany and France)

Nocturne No. 13 in D minor — 1834 (France)

Nocturne No. 14 in C — *1836 (France and Austria)

*According to Grattan Flood published by Clementi, Collard and Collard in 1822, but a review a year earlier makes Cecil Hopkinson place its publication as 1821.

Nocturne No. 15 in C	*1836 (France and Austria)
Nocturne No. 16 in F (this having a Quintet form also)	*1836 (France and Austria)
	*These editions spread through agents in Russia and London.
Sehnsüchts-Walzer (E major)	First known edition 1845 (Germany), likely earlier first printing
Andante Inédit in E flat	1852 (Russia)
La Danse des Ours (Piano Solo version, C major)	1912 (Germany, in Heinrich Dessauer's *John Field*)
Largo (C minor)	1961 (photographic facsimile of MS in Cecil Hopkinson's *Thematic Catalogue*)
Nocturne in B flat	− − − (Russia, in a musical magazine)
88 Passages, *doigtés par lui même* (from Concertos and other works)	− − − (Russia)

Works mentioned by various writers, but their content unknown or conjectural − − − including published (but either no certain date or no supporting reference) and MS:

Nocturne, *Dernière Pensée*
Pastorale − − − after the MS of Field's pupil Reinhardt (question: the very short solo version of the *Grande Pastorale* copied by Reinhardt)
Logie of Buchan Rondo (announced 1799, but untraced)
Slave, Bear the Sparkling Goblet Round (published, but lost)
Go to the Devil and Shake Yourself (published, but lost)
Piano Concerto No. 8
An Impromptu on a Handel theme (untraced, mentioned in the St. Petersburg News as published 1813, dedicated Marshall Kutusoff, Prince Smolenski, brave officers and Russian Army, by Field) is more likely to be an error for Cramer's Impromptu in G, *Kutusoff's Victory*, on Handel's air *Disdainful of Danger*, with that dedication.

Other works in MS, such as the solo versions of further Concerto movements mentioned in the text and of the A flat Quintet − − − it could be possible for the list to be considerably extended as more of these come to light.

Bibliography.

Abraham, Gerald *Chopin's Musical Style* (London, 1939)

Benyovszky, Károly *J. N. Hummel, der Mensch und Künstler* (Bratislava, 1934)

Boucourechliev, Andre *Chopin − − − a pictorial biography* (London, 1963)

Bourniquel, Camille *Chopin* (New York; London, 1960)

Capon, Charles L. *John Field: in Famous Composers and Their Works* (Boston, U.S.A., 1891)

Chissell, Joan *Chopin* (London, 1963)

Davey, Henry *History of English Music* (London, 1895)

Dessauer, Heinrich *John Field, sein Leben und seine Werke* (Langensalza, 1912)

Deutsch, Otto Erich *Musikverlags Nummern* (Berlin, 1961)

Einstein, Alfred *A Short History of Music* (London, 1936)

Flood, W. H. Grattan *John Field of Dublin: Inventor of the Nocturne−A Brief Memoir* (Dublin, 1921)

Hadden, J. Cuthbert *Chopin* (Master Musicians Series, London, 1903)

Harasowski, Adam *The Skein of Legends around Chopin* (Glasgow, 1967)

Hedley, Arthur *Chopin* (Master Musicians Series, London, 1947)

Hedley, Arthur *Selected Correspondences of Fryderyck Chopin* (London, 1962)

Hopkinson, Cecil *A Bibliographical Thematic Catalogue of the Works of John Field* (Bath, 1961)

Karasowski, Moritz *Chopin* (London, 1879)

Kelly, Edgar Stillman *Chopin the Composer* (New York, 1913)

Lang, Paul Henry *Music in Western Civilization* (New York, 1941)

Liszt, Franz *On John Field's Nocturnes − − − Introductory Essay to his first edition of these* (Leipzig, 1859)

Maine, Basil *Chopin* (London, 1933)

Mizwa, Stephen P. *Chopin* (New York, 1949)

Niecks, Frederick *Frederick Chopin as a Man and Musician* (London, 1888)

Nikolaev, Alexandr A. *John Field* (Moscow, 1960)

Porte, John. F. *Chopin the Composer and his Music* (London, 1932)

Riemann, Hugo *Musiklexicon* (Germany, *editions 1882–1969*)

Schonberg, Harold C. *The Great Pianists* (London, 1964)

Schumann, Robert *Music and Musicians* (London, 1877–80)

Spohr, Louis *Autobiography* (Germany, 1860; London, 1885)

Walker, Alan *Frédéric Chopin: profiles of the man and the musician* (London, 1966)

Walker, Ernest *A History of Music in England* (Oxford, 1907; 3rd edition, 1952)

Weinstock, Herbert *Chopin − − − The Man and his Music* (New York, 1949)

Wierzynski, Casimir *The Life and Death of Chopin* (New York, 1951)

Articles by:

Foss, Hubert *on Chopin Centenary* in *Radio Times*

Fox, Charles *to accompany start of series of Chopin broadcasts,* in *Radio Times*

and in:

Grove's Dictionary of Music and Musicians

Men of Music (U.S.A.)

Musical Times − − − on Chopin Centenary

Encyclopaedia Britannica

Routledge's Encyclopaedia